# CUSTOMERS FROM AFAR

"Happiness is having a friend from afar."
— *Confucius*

## YOUR KEY TO SERVING CHINESE CONSUMERS

Raymond Ng

A S.U.C.C.E.S.S. Publication

The publisher gratefully acknowledges Asia Pacific Foundation of
Canada  and ParkLane Ventures Ltd. PARKLANE
for their sponsorship and support.

❦

Copyright © 1996 by Raymond Ng

A S.U.C.C.E.S.S. Publication
United Chinese Community Enrichment Services Society
87 East Pender Street, Vancouver, British Columbia  V6A 1S9

ISBN 1-896148-08-5
Printed in Canada
First edition:  May, 1996

**Canadian Cataloguing in Publication Data**

Ng, Raymond, 1947 -
    Customers from afar

Includes bibliographical references and index.
ISBN 1-896148-08-5
1. Chinese Canadian consumers.* 2. Marketing—Canada.  I.
S.U.C.C.E.S.S.  II. Title.
HF5415.33.C3N5 1996        658.8'348        C96-910134-1

Project Manager: Thomas Tam
Research Coordinator: Kelly Ng
Production Coordinator: Lily Chan
Editor: Nancy Knickerbocker
Cover Design / Page Layout: Jackie Liu
Cover Illustration: Peter Mong
Computer Production: AdCity Graphics Group

Your

Key

to

Serving

Chinese

Consumers

Chinese calligraphy: *yī* (upper right) means clothing; *shí* (lower right) means food; *zhù* (upper left) means accommodation; and *xíng* (lower left) means transportation. When used together, these characters mean all the daily necessities.

(Calligraphy by Tsang Yee Leung)

# Contents

## Part III -  Meeting and Networking
## with Your Customers

*For my parents,*
*for giving me a proud heritage,*
*and for Nancy, Jonathan and Joycelin,*
*for carrying on the legacy.*

# Foreword

The twenty-first century will be an era of global interdependence. It will be an era when no single country, culture or economy can thrive in isolation, when diversity is a necessary ingredient for success. As more and more people from all around the world are making Canada their new home, this country is quickly becoming a leader in the global multicultural economy of tomorrow.

As we approach the threshold of the next millennium, signs of global interdependence are springing up everywhere: the unification of Europe, the rise of the Asian economy, the Internet, the North American Free Trade Agreement. Humankind can no longer think in terms of traditional boundaries. As Canadians, we must embrace the world and think in multicultural terms. Canadians of all origins should not measure each other by numbers, but should contribute their talents and the richness of their heritage to this wonderful society. We need to understand and learn from each other by opening dialogues, exchanging views, recognizing each other's concerns and celebrating our differences.

We also need to extend our welcome and assistance to new citizens. These new Canadians have taken a courageous step by leaving their homelands behind in order to join us. As newcomers they have concerns other Canadians may not have experienced or may have long forgotten. They are helping us build this country; let us help them build a new home.

I am pleased to announce the arrival of this book, which deals with the vital topic of cross-cultural marketing. This book is about the opportunities presented by one of Canada's visible minorities: the Chinese Canadians, many of whom are new citizens. It provides a tool for Canadians to understand, on a practical level, the needs, concerns and values of a particular people, a people who have contributed to Canada's development since pioneer days. Although the content is specific to one cultural group, the spirit can extend to all others. I encourage fellow Canadians to apply the same spirit of understanding and make similar attempts to cover the needs and concerns of citizens of other cultural heritage.

Dr. David C. Lam
C.V.O., O.C., K.St.J.
LL.D.,D.H.L.,D.Mil.Sc.,D.H.
Former Lieutenant-Governor of B.C.

# $\mathscr{A}$cknowledgements

$M$ore minds have contributed to this book than I have room to say. I am grateful to countless individuals from corporate executives to students who have donated both time and effort.

I am especially indebted to BC TEL for many reasons. In 1994, BC TEL started an intensive effort to bring its services to Chinese customers. As a part of this effort, I took part in the training of hundreds of its employees, many of whom have given me wonderful feedback and insights. The dedication of this workforce and their desire to serve the customers across cultural differences are the main sources of inspiration for me. I am further indebted to BC TEL for permitting me to use the name of their course, "Customers From Afar," which I helped to develop, as the title of this book. Two individuals, in particular, have contributed greatly to this project: Thomas Leung, Director of International Market, for his time and information, and Lee Clements-Nazarali, Training Manager, for her unfailing support.

Writing of this book would not have been possible without the dedication and hard work of the staff at the United Chinese Community Enrichment Services Society (S.U.C.C.E.S.S.) I am especially grateful to Chairman Mason Loh for his encouragement and valuable feedback, to Lilian To, Executive Director, for the information and resources she provided, to Thomas Tam for managing this project, to Kelly Ng, Centina Lowe, Mary Kam and David Ho for their thorough research, to Lily Chan and Clara Kwan for coordinating the production, marketing and administrative details.

Much of the marketing information on Chinese Canadians was supplied by DJC Research. I am grateful especially to Dan Colquhoun, President of DJC, for sharing the very valuable information with the readers, for validating the content on marketing information, and for his input and feedback.

My special gratitude to the following individuals who willingly shared their stories and contributed a great deal of their time: Tung Chan, Vice President - Asian Banking of the Toronto Dominion Bank, also former Deputy Mayor of the City of Vancouver; Alfred Chu, Y. M. Kwong and K.K. Lau, three new Chinese Canadians; Rhonda Margolis, a training consultant on cross-cultural issues; Bob Rennie, Principal of Ulinder Rennie Project Marketing; Dr. Jan Walls, Professor, David Lam Centre for International Communication, Simon Fraser University; and Peeter Wesig, President of ParkLane Ventures Ltd. In addition to sharing their viewpoints, Ms. Margolis and Dr. Walls also helped to validate the content of this book.

A lot of marketing experts have also contributed their knowledge and time. Many thanks to Anthony Chow and John Philip Ho of Colorama Productions Inc.; to Sonny Wong of Hamazaki Wong Marketing Group, who is also a columnist for *Business in Vancouver*; and to the staff of LLT Marketing, especially Frieda Ng, Bonnie Soo, Risa Liu and Benny Wan.

Many people in sales also helped out with practical tips on serving customers. I am especially grateful to these individuals for the enormous amount of time they put in: Allan deGenova of

D'Ovidio DeGenova Marketing; Antony Towe of Sutton Group-Langara Realty; Chris Kayat of Realty World - Riverside; and Patrick Ho of Countryside Realty.

A book like this requires special expertise from many different areas. I am deeply indebted to economist Don DeVoretz and business strategist Caroline Smart, both professors at Simon Fraser University. I am also indebted to Timothy Shen, President of the Canada China Trade Development Association and to Wilfred Wong, investment consultant at Richardson Greenshield of Canada, for their valuable opinions.

My view on cross-cultural business practices would have been grossly inadequate if it were not for the ideas from these cultural consultants: Steven Cheng of Orientalia Enterprises; Celia Lam; Loretta Lam of Focus Communications; and Nancy Li.

Various media also offered extremely valuable information and help. My thanks to Joe Chan of Fairchild TV; Anthony Choi of Trillium Communications; George Froehlich of CKVU-UTV; Wayne Gooding of the Financial Post Magazine; John Hui and Alvin Au of the Chinese Capital Business Magazine; Hanson Lau of Mainstream Broadcasting Corporation; Eric Wong of the *Ming Pao* Newspaper and Terence Wong of Canadian Chinese Radio. All of them have taken a great deal of time from their very busy schedules to give their views on a range of issues.

I am also indebted to the many people who took part in focus group meetings. My special thanks go to the employees of these firms whose input forms the core of this book: The Brick Warehouse Corporation, Middlegate Honda, ParkLane Ventures Ltd., Realty World Coronation West and VanCity Credit Union.

I am honoured that a number of world-class photographers have contributed to the book. Readers will find a photo credit beside each picture to identify each individual's work. Their photographic artistry has added much life to the text, and I thank them all most sincerely.

Last but not least, I would like to thank my editor, Nancy Knickerbocker, for her opinions and for making this book a lot more readable.

# Introduction

Imagine serving 800,000 ready, willing and able customers, who are easy and inexpensive to reach, who will refer other customers to you after the sale, and whose number is growing by leaps and bounds. Now stop imagining. These customers are waiting for you to make a move. This book will tell you how.

Few people living in Toronto or Vancouver will dispute the change of ethnic mix in these two cities over the last decade. It does not take a statistician to notice the dramatic increase in the number of Asian faces, especially the Chinese. To most business people, the population change implies a change in their customer base. It also implies a change in customers' preferences, and possibly, a need to adjust the way business is done.

Most Chinese people in Canada came from Hong Kong, Taiwan, or mainland China, although they could have come from anywhere in the world. For the past ten years, Hong Kong has consistently been the top source of immigrants to Canada, with China and Taiwan ranking in the top five. Regardless of where they come from, the Chinese continue to immigrate to Canada in large numbers. The Chinese Canadian population grew dramatically from about 267,000 in 1986 to about 856,000 in 1995.[1] If this rate of growth continues unabated, by the turn of the century the Chinese Canadian population will likely reach 1.2 million.

More than two-thirds of the Chinese in Canada live in metropolitan Toronto or Vancouver. In 1994, Chinese population of Toronto was estimated to be more than 300,000, whereas that of

1

Vancouver was more than 200,000.[2] Both estimates are regarded to be very conservative. Some undocumented estimates have put the figures between 50,000 to 100,000 higher for both cities.

The impact of the Chinese as a consumer group in these two cities is visible everywhere, reaching far beyond the limits of the traditional Chinatowns. Chinese signs can be seen from most street corners. Dozens of first-class shopping centres were opened by the Chinese, displaying merchandise tailored to the Chinese life-styles. Many business people, from home builders to automobile retailers, have credited much of the recent growth of their business to the new immigrants. As market researcher Dan Colquhoun noted: "Suddenly, a market was born."[3]

Every newcomer to this country needs to set up a home, to move around, to communicate with others, to handle their financial affairs, to educate and clothe their children, and the list goes on. Economist Don DeVoretz of Simon Fraser University, who specializes in immigration economics, predicted that over the next ten years, most sectors related to household operations will continue to do well due to immigration. For example, over the past five years, an average immigrant from Hong Kong spent $100,000 in his first year of settlement.[4] Arriving at a rate of 30,000 to 40,000 a year, people from Hong Kong alone are injecting $3 to $4 billion a year into the Canadian economy. Presumably, much of the cash is initially absorbed by those sectors related to the setting up and operation of households.

The Chinese segment, being the largest group of newcomers, will take up a good share of the consumption pie. According to Sampling Research and Technologies Inc., consumption by Chinese today accounts for 7.4% of the purchasing power in the combined Toronto, Vancouver and Montreal markets, up from 5.3% in 1991. By 2000, Chinese will account for 10.2% of the purchasing power. Judging from the population growth, this growth in purchasing power is hardly surprising.

Most Chinese people live in certain areas within metropolitan Toronto and Vancouver. They like to visit certain types of places, and get their information from certain ethnic media. Their closely knit social infrastructure allows news to travel very efficiently. This means the Chinese people as a group of consumers are easy to reach. Many marketers have also found this segment remarkably inexpensive to target. Details of their population distribution and available media can be found in Part II of this book.

In many ways, Chinese customers are no different from other customers. They have the same needs as any other consumer new to the country. They expect to get the best value for the dollars they pay. They have a need to communicate and be understood. They value quality products, responsible service and long term relationships. They may speak different languages and belong to a different culture, but they share many of the same needs and dreams of other Canadians. Therefore serving the Chinese does not require a drastically different approach. All it takes is a marketer's common sense, as well as your sensitivity to your customer's feelings. "It comes down to basic respect for your customers," says marketer Bob Rennie of Ulinder Rennie Project Marketing Corporation.

Although the focus of this book is serving Chinese Canadians as consumers, the economic opportunities they present go far beyond marketing and consumption. In fact, the same economic opportunities are presented by all other ethnic groups. Together, they are continually creating niche markets that were not there before. They bring in capital and skills of all kinds to the Canadian economy. As consumers, their demands encourage competition, which in turn raises the quality of goods and services. Many of our new immigrants are proven entrepreneurs with excellent business networks. Their presence in our communities means Canadians no longer have to travel abroad before we can meet and make friends from other cultures.

A mistake suppliers sometimes make in approaching Chinese customers is to view them more as a cultural group than a consumer group. In so doing they often concentrate on relating to them on a cultural level instead of trying to meet their needs. This approach not only misses the point but may come across as patronizing to many customers. The purpose of this book is to emphasize the consumer needs and behaviours of Chinese Canadians, and to show suppliers how to meet their needs within the context of their culture and lifestyle.

Another mistake suppliers may make is to ignore the diversity among the Chinese people. Worldwide, one out of five people is a Chinese, and China is almost as large and diverse as Europe. The Chinese people in Canada came from all parts of the world. They belong to different ethnic groups and speak different dialects. The only thing that binds them together is their common heritage.

Linked by this common heritage, the Chinese Canadians have over the years developed their own infrastructure. Serving

Chinese Canadians well means understanding and bridging into their infrastructure, not just recognizing a few perceived symbols of ethnic behaviour. You must be prepared to invest time and resources to develop this bridge. This book will provide some advice on how to channel resources to this end.

## About this book

This book is the results of ten months of interviews and surveys involving individuals and focus groups from a cross section of Chinese Canadians. While these studies provided an indication of the way many Chinese consumers behave, they were not designed to give a precise picture definable in statistical terms. Describing their consumer behaviours with precision can be very difficult. Not only are the Chinese a very diverse group of people, their behaviour patterns are also constantly changing. In a very real way, the current Chinese Canadian population is a population in transition. Describing their behavioural patterns is like describing the location of a moving target. On the other hand, as a population, they share a common culture. As newcomers to this country, they share a common set of needs. As such, studies about their cultural and behavioural patterns, albeit changing, will still be useful.

Unlike other books on Chinese culture, the focus of this book is on the Chinese people in Canada as a consumer group. Its purpose is to help the business community serve the Chinese consumer group in Canada. While both cultural and business issues will be covered, this is not a book about the Chinese culture, or about how to do business in China. I have included a list of references for those interested in further reading in these areas.

In a book like this, it is necessary to compare Chinese Canadian consumers with mainstream consumers. The difficulty lies in how such comparisons can be made without running the risk of stereotyping. Each group is very diverse. Probably there is just as much diversity within each group as there is between the two. Whenever comparison is made, one should always see it as two bell curves placed side by side with a good deal of overlap. Remember that among the Chinese Canadians there are many whose behaviour is indistinguishable from the majority of other Canadians. At the same time, I have also met many non-Chinese whose knowledge of Chinese culture and language surpasses that of some people born into the culture. As an example, the academic consultant for the sections of this book relating to Chinese culture is Dr. Jan Walls, a Caucasian expert on Asian cultures.

Most Chinese Canadians speak Mandarin, Cantonese, or both. At the present time, there are more people speaking Cantonese than Mandarin in Canada. Worldwide, however, Mandarin is the predominant Chinese dialect by a wide margin. It is also fast gaining popularity in Canada. For this reason, I will use Mandarin as the basis of all Chinese words in this book, and the *pīn yīn* system for their phonetic representations. *Pīn yīn* is a commonly accepted phonetic system in China. Although there are some differences between *pīn yīn* and the English phonetics, especially for symbols such as *q* and *x*, it is by far the most "English-like" phonetic system available to represent Chinese words. Readers interested in pronouncing the Chinese words can refer to explanations of the *pīn yīn* system in the Appendix.

Where appropriate, I have also included phonetic translations of words in Cantonese. Such occurrence will be specified in the text so that readers will not confuse a Cantonese with a Mandarin translation. In representing the sounds of Cantonese words, I have simply followed the English phonetic system, which is no better or worse than any other system for this purpose.

## Use of terms

*Chinese Canadians:* This term refers to all the people of Chinese origin living in Canada, including the native born, immigrants and naturalized citizens.

*Customers:* The word customers will be used throughout to mean Chinese customers. This narrow definition of the word is adopted strictly for the purpose of reducing verbiage, and should not be construed as an intent to exclude customers of other cultural heritage. Where the broader sense of the word is intended, it will be specified in the text.

*He/she:* Recognizing the growing number of women in business today, I began by using he/she throughout, but found this phrasing very cumbersome. I trust female readers will understand that the traditional male personal pronoun is used simply for brevity.

## A word for our American readers

Although this book is written in Canada about Chinese Canadians, much of the information on culture and consumer behaviours is applicable to the Chinese population in the USA. Americans only need to substitute the term Chinese Americans for Chinese Canadians and much of the information will still be valid. In many ways, the situation with respect to Asian Pacific Americans (APA) is very similar to that for Asian Pacific Canadians.

## *Celebrate our diversity*

I have spent the last 28 years of my life in various parts of Canada. Throughout the years I have observed both the turmoil and the economic miracles on Asian soil, the waves of immigrants in search of a better home, their joy and sorrow in this wonderful country, and the very positive steps Canadians have made to receive them into this land. I have also seen very unnecessary misunderstandings on both sides due to miscommunication and false assumptions, which stifle business and create counter-productive social tension.

My ultimate goal in writing this book is to facilitate understanding between Chinese and other Canadians. There are many ways to achieve this goal. I have chosen to address the issue from a business angle because it provides a practical way to look at our common ground. Through buying and selling we can find out how much the two groups of citizens need each other to survive, to prosper and to live out our common dream.

---

[1] Derived from 1991 Census, Statistics Canada, Catalogue 93-315, and immigration information from Citizenship and Immigration Canada.

[2] "The Chinese Consumer in Canada." Toronto: DJC Research, 1994.

[3] Colquhoun, Daniel. "The Chinese Consumer in Canada — a World of Opportunity." Multicultural Marketing Symposium, December 1, 1994, Vancouver, BC.

[4] Wong, Sonny. "Wake up and smell the tea." *Business in Vancouver*, November 16-22, 1993, Issue #212.

# Part I

# *K*nowing Your Customers

*"Winning involves knowing yourself and others."*

— Sun Tzu, an ancient Chinese military strategist

# *I*ntroduction to Part I

When a famous Japanese automobile manufacturer decided to open the market in Spain, one of the first things management did was to send a senior officer to the country for a year. His mission was to learn about Spanish guitar. To most Westerners, cars and music have little in common. The Japanese, however, look at it in a different way. They feel before a supplier enters into a new market, he needs to study everything he can about the culture and way of life of the people who will be buying the product.

Learning about the customers' culture and way of life makes good business sense. Serving customers means meeting their needs. Meeting a person's needs starts with understanding what those needs are. When the customers and suppliers belong to the same cultural background, it is easy for the suppliers to recognize the customers' needs. When they belong to different cultures, a great deal of learning is required before the suppliers can see the consumer needs the way the customers see them.

Learning about someone else's culture is not easy. It involves challenging assumptions a person has held since childhood, opening up to new ideas and constructing new relevance from concepts that are not normally a part of ourselves. Part I is about building the foundation for this new relevance. It offers six chapters of the cultural basics, and should be read by anyone who has an interest in serving the Chinese consumers in this country.

Chapter One presents the Chinese history and civilization in a nutshell. When I first started this project, I pondered for a long time whether to include a short chapter on Chinese history. On one hand, I am not sure how applicable Chinese history is to today's Canadian marketplace. On the other hand, it is fair to say that one does not truly understand the Chinese people unless he understands the significance of history to them. History is an integral part of the Chinese culture. Just as a Chinese individual cannot think of himself outside the context of his family, the Chinese people cannot think of themselves outside the context of their 5,000 years of history. To the Chinese people, history is heritage. For this reason, I have decided to include the chapter. Although it is possible to skip this chapter in its entirety and still understand the rest of the book, the chapter contains the historical root of much of the information you will read in later chapters.

Chapter Two gives a brief overview of Hong Kong, Taiwan and mainland China, the three places from which most Chinese Canadians came. Reading this chapter will give you an idea of the way of life of many Chinese Canadians before they came to this country.

Chapter Three describes some of the challenges facing new Canadians as they adjust socially in the host country. This is a very important chapter because it allows suppliers to see things through the eyes of new immigrants. It also underlines the importance of distinguishing transient behaviours immigrants used to cope with changes from permanent cultural behaviours.

Chapter Four discusses three fundamental differences between Chinese and Western cultural concepts: the emphasis on harmony, types of social relationships and communication patterns. Information in this chapter will help readers understand some of the behaviours and unspoken concerns many Chinese people have in social interchange.

Chapter Five describes the various types of beliefs among the Chinese people. The information in this chapter can help readers understand some of the buyers' preferences that are based upon religious beliefs.

Chapter Six is about Chinese festivals. It describes three major festivals and the business opportunities they provide.

These soldiers are a small part of a terra cotta army unearthed recently in Xīan, China. They stood guard at the tomb of Shǐ Huángdì for more than 2,000 years.

(Photo courtesy of Kiu Chan)

# Chapter One

# *C*hinese History and Civilization

## *A well-cultured people*

"Perhaps the single most important fact Chinese people want others to recognize is that they are a well-cultured people by world standard," according to Dr. Jan Walls, a professor of Asian Studies at the David Lam Centre of Simon Fraser University.

For thousands of years, the Chinese civilization was, in many ways, the most developed of the time. The word "China" in Chinese, *Zhōng Guó*, means "the Middle Kingdom." Today most Chinese no longer see themselves as the people in the middle of the world, but it would be wrong to see the Chinese civilization as under-developed. Unfortunately, one of the most common mistakes people make is to equate cultural with economic development. Since China is still a developing country in economic terms, many people tend to see the Chinese as people from a culturally under-developed country. What they fail to see is the struggle China had to face over the last 100 years, when colonialism, wars and internal turmoil reduced the once-mighty nation to near economic disaster. Only recently has China been given the time to recover. Yet in war or peace, in prosperity or poverty, the Chinese civilization continues to develop and blossom in its own way. This is an extremely important fact to bear in mind when one is

15

dealing with Chinese people.  Nothing is further from the truth and more insulting to the Chinese than to regard them as coming from a sub-standard civilization.

China has over 5,000 years of continuous history,  and is the longest living civilization in the world to date.  Its long history has made its past an inseparable part of the Chinese identity.  There are many books on Chinese history.  The reference section at the end of this chapter only provides a partial list.  This chapter will give a *very* brief summary of what happened in China in the past 5,000 years.

## Origin of Chinese civilization

Historians cannot agree on exactly when the Chinese civilization began, for people have lived in China long before there were any written records.  What is not in dispute is that China was one of the four cradles of civilization.  Early evidence indicates the existence of at least two sophisticated agricultural communities in the valley of the Yellow River by as early as 10,000 B.C.  Some Chinese works of art, including pottery and carved jades, date from the 5000's B.C.  The earliest walled town, uncovered at Lóng-quán Zhèn, can be dated back to 3500 B.C.

By the Second Millennium B.C., China already had its first urban civilization, the Bronze Age culture of the Shāng Dynasty (c.1766-c.1122 B.C.).  The Shāng Dynasty was a very well developed society governed by aristocrats.  It is famous for its bronze vessels and pictorial symbols, an early form of Chinese writing, scratched on bones.  Other civilizations that flourished in the ancient world include the towns and villages in Mesopotamia, the

Nile and the Indus. All of these were farming communities located in broad river valleys.

## *The First Millennium, B.C.*

Shortly before the First Millennium, B.C., the Shāng Dynasty was replaced by the Zhōu Dynasty (c.1122-c.256 B.C.). In theory, the Zhōu Dynasty lasted for almost 900 years. In practice, however, the rulers of the Zhōu Dynasty never gained complete control of China. From its very beginning, the Zhōu rulers delegated much of the local authority to certain loyal followers, who later turned the land they controlled into semi-independent states that rivalled against each other. The Zhōu government itself turned from a weakened to a token government, and by 256 B.C., it ceased to exist. China became an open battlefield for seven independent states.

The Zhōu Dynasty and the ensuing warring period was a time of great cultural accomplishment. There were many scholars, philosophers, military strategists, statesmen and orators. The work of many of these people has been studied and admired for centuries after they died. For example, the system of moral values and responsible behaviours, proposed by philosopher Confucius around 500 B.C., has immense influence on Chinese behaviour even today. The teachings of Lǎo Zi (Lǎo Tzu) (605-520 B.C.), founder of Daoism (also known as Taoism), formed the basis of many Chinese beliefs for 2,000 years. Other works of great significance that were developed in the period include *Yì Jìng (I Ching*, or the Book of Changes), and *The Art of War*. *Yì Jìng*, originally developed as a systematic method to predict the future, is still

17

A view of the Great Wall of China. Spanning 7,400 km, the Wall is the only man-made object visible from outer space.
(Photo courtesy of Mathew Leung)

used by scholars and philosophers throughout the world. *The Art of War*, a classic of military strategies written by Sūn Zi (Sun Tzu), is now used in a number of applications, most notably in business for insights into strategic planning and negotiation. More information on the ideas and concepts of Confucius and Lǎo Zi (Lǎo Tzu) can be found in Chapter Five.

The Period of the Warring States eventually ended in 221 B.C., about 100 years after Alexander the Great conquered Asia Minor, when the state of Qín conquered all other states and established the first empire with a strong central government. The ruler of Qín then declared himself to be Shǐ Huángdì (The First Emperor). The Qín Dynasty lasted only 15 years, but it accomplished a great deal through tyranny and strict laws. One of its greatest achievements was the linking up of a number of fortifications to form the famous Great Wall of China. Measuring 7,400 kilometres, the wall protected China for many centuries. It also standardized the measuring system, the monetary system, and the writing system.

Shortly after the death of the First Emperor, the Qín Dynasty collapsed. The Hàn Dynasty gained control of China in 202 B.C. and ruled China for the next four centuries. During this millennium in other parts of the world, many empires also came and vanished. Notably were the Assyrian Empire, the Babylonian Empire, the rise of Alexander the Great, and the Maurya Empire in India. China was still under the rule of the Hàn Dynasty when Christ was born. Highlights of this millennium include:

c.1000 B.C.      King David united Israel and Judah

c.671 B.C.      Assyrians conquered Egypt

| c.625-539 B.C. | Nebuchadnessar ruled the New Babylonian Empire |
| **c.605 B.C.** | **Lǎo Zi (Lǎo Tzu) was born** |
| c.563 B.C. | Siddhartha Gautama (Buddha) was born |
| **c.551 B.C.** | **Confucius was born** |
| c.539-330 B.C. | Darius I built the Persian Empire |
| c.387 B.C. | Plato founded the Academy in Athens |
| c.334-325 B.C. | Alexander the Great conquered Asia Minor and Egypt |
| c.320-185 B.C. | The Maurya Empire united all of India |
| **c.256 B.C.** | **End of Zhōu Dynasty in China** |
| **c.221 B.C.** | **The First Emperor Shǐ Huángdì unified China** |
| **c.202 B.C.** | **The Hàn Dynasty began in China** |
| c.58-49 B.C. | Julius Caesar conquered much of Europe and the Mediterranean |
| c.4 B.C. | Jesus Christ was born |

## The First Millennium

For a few hundred years during this millennium, two empires dominated the world: the Chinese and the Romans. Later with the rise of the Muslim civilization, a third power was added onto the world's map.

In China, the millennium began in the middle of the Hàn Dynasty (202 B.C. to A.D. 220). The Hàn Dynasty expanded the Chinese empire into Central Asia. It adopted Confucianism as the philosophical basis of government, and saw the first major history of China written. There was also a great deal of development in the field of science. For example, paper was invented

20

during this time. A land trade route, later known as the Silk Road, was developed, linking China with Europe for the first time.

Civil war broke out by the end of the Hàn Dynasty, and China was split into three competing kingdoms. This civil war was followed quickly by the invasion of nomadic groups from the north. For the next three to four centuries, China was both divided and ruled by a series of short-lived kingdoms and dynasties. During this period, Buddhism had a great influence in China. Science and technology also flourished. This chaotic period ended in A.D. 581 when the Suí Dynasty re-united China again.

The Suí Dynasty (581-618) was also short-lived. Its greatest contribution was the construction of the Grand Canal that connected northern China with the Yāngzi (Yangtze) River. Though constructed at great cost, the canal facilitated trade between the north and south for centuries to come.

The Táng Dynasty (618-907) replaced the Suí, and provided China with almost three centuries of prosperity. This is a period when the Chinese civilization reached another new height. Some of the greatest poets lived in this period. Gunpowder, the wheelbarrow and the blast furnace were invented. In its heyday, the capital Chang'an (today Xi'an) was the largest city on the planet. With a population of more than a million people, it attracted traders from as far away as the Mediterranean. The Táng Dynasty was so splendid that even now the Chinese people still identify themselves as the Táng people. The dynasty ended in A.D.907 after a series of rebellions. China once again broke up into a number of local governments until the Sòng Dynasty reunified the country in A.D. 960.

While China went from the Hàn to the Sòng Dynasty, else-where in the world, a number of significant events also took place, such as the splitting up of the Roman Empire, the rule of north-ern India under the Gupta Dynasty, the rise of Islam, and the expansion of the Byzantine Empire. Some events in this millen-nium are:

| | |
|---|---|
| A.D. 30 | Jesus Christ was crucified |
| A.D. 96-180 | The Roman Empire reached its height of power and prosperity |
| **A.D. 220** | **Fall of the Hàn Dynasty in China. Beginning of The Three Kingdoms.** |
| A.D. 330 | Constantine made Byzantium (Constantinople) capital of the Roman Empire |
| A.D. 395 | The Roman Empire split into West and East |
| A.D. 476 | Fall of West Roman Empire, beginning of the Middle Ages |
| A.D. 320-500 | Gupta Dynasty ruled northern India |
| A.D. 570 | Mohammed was born |
| **A.D. 581** | **Suí Dynasty reunified China** |
| **A.D. 618** | **Beginning of Táng Dynasty in China** |
| A.D. 622 | Mohammed's *Hegira* took place, Islamic Era began |
| A.D. 632 | Mohammed died. Expansion of the Muslim world began |
| A.D. 800 | Charlemagne crowned Emperor of the Romans by Pope Leo III |
| A.D. 867 | Basil I began expanding the Byzantine (East Roman) Empire |
| **A.D. 907** | **Fall of the Táng Dynasty in China** |
| **A.D. 960** | **Beginning of the Sòng Dynasty in China** |

## The Second Millennium

The Sòng Dynasty (960-1279) ruled China for more than 300 years. During its reign, two significant changes were introduced that affected China for the next 1,000 years. First was the re-establishment of the civil examination that had been introduced during the Táng Dynasty. This examination was a system whereby officials were selected on the basis of knowledge instead of ancestry. The introduction of this system provided a more practical incentive for people to study than being able to understand the thoughts of the sages. The second was the adoption of neo-Confucianism as the official philosophy. Neo-Confucianism was largely founded by philosopher Zhū Xī, who integrated traditional Confucian values with elements of Buddhism and Daoism. More information about these three schools of thought can be found in Chapter Five.

The Sòng Dynasty was frequently attacked by the northern nomads. By 1127, invaders from Manchuria had gained control of northern China. In the 1200's, Mongol warriors defeated all nomads and the Sòng Dynasty, and founded the Yuán Dynasty.

The Yuán Dynasty (1279-1368) lasted less than a century, and was part of the vast Mongol Empire that extended from eastern Europe to Korea. Many foreigners visited China during this period. Most notably was Marco Polo from Venice, who wrote extensively about his experience in China. Unwilling to withstand the Mongols' harsh rule, the Chinese people overthrew them and established the Míng Dynasty.

The Míng Dynasty (1368-1644) provided China with more than two hundred years of stability. While the Míng government encouraged the development of art and literature, it discouraged trading with European countries. During this period, Christopher Columbus landed in America (1492), followed by the landing of the first British settlers on the New World (1607). The Míng government was gradually weakened by corrupt officials and eunuchs (servants to the emperors). In the end, it was overthrown by a group of bandits.

After the fall of the Míng Dynasty, the Manchus from Manchuria quickly moved in to gain control of China. They established the Qīng Dynasty in 1644, and ruled China until 1911. The Manchus adopted the Míng's political model, and supported neo-Confucianism, thereby winning the support of the scholars. They also expanded into Mongolia, Tibet and central Asia. By the 1800's, however, the empire was much weakened by uncontrolled population growth, corruption and rebellions. It also adopted a closed-door policy which isolated China from the rest of the world.

In the meantime, the Western world also was going through dramatic changes. In North America, the colonists declared independence from Britain. Europe saw the rise and fall of Napoleon. The Industrial Revolution was in high gear. A number of European nations, notably Britain and France, began expanding their territories worldwide. By the middle of the nineteenth century, almost every Western power wanted a piece of territory in China. Japan too went through a major reform. Between 1842 and 1895, the Qīng government lost a series of wars to the Western powers and Japan, giving up more and more rights and territories. China was on the verge of being divided by foreign powers.

In 1911, a revolution took place. The next year, the last emperor of the Qīng Dynasty gave up his throne. The Republic of China was formed. More information about what happened after the forming of the Republic can be found in Chapter Two.

The one thousand years between the Sòng Dynasty and the present was a time of great changes throughout the world. Some key events:

| | |
|---|---|
| A.D. 1231 | Roman Catholic Church established the Inquisition |
| **A.D. 1279** | **Kublai Khan conquered China, beginning of Yuán Dynasty** |
| **A.D. 1368** | **End of Yuán Dynasty, beginning of Míng Dynasty** |
| A.D. 1438 | The Hapsburgs began to rule the Holy Roman Empire |
| A.D. 1453 | The Ottomans captured Constantinople, Byzantine Empire collapsed |
| A.D. 1492 | Christopher Columbus landed in America |
| A.D. 1517 | Martin Luther issued Ninety-five Theses |
| A.D. 1607 | First British settlement in North America established |
| A.D. 1618 | Thirty Years' War began |
| **A.D. 1644** | **Beginning of Qīng Dynasty in China** |
| A.D. 1769 | James Watt developed an efficient steam engine |
| A.D. 1776 | Colonists declared independence from Britain, USA was formed |
| A.D. 1789 | Outbreak of the French Revolution |
| A.D. 1815 | Napoleon defeated at Waterloo |
| **A.D. 1842** | **China ceded Hong Kong to Britain** |
| A.D. 1861-1865 | Civil War in USA |

| | |
|---|---|
| A.D. 1867 | The British North America Act established the Dominion of Canada |
| A.D. 1876 | Alexander Graham Bell invented the telephone |
| **A.D. 1911** | **Beginning of Republic of China** |
| A.D. 1914-22 | World War I |
| A.D. 1939-45 | World War II |
| A.D. 1947 | India gained independence from Britain |
| **A.D. 1949** | **People's Republic of China began, Kaomintang retreated to Taiwan** |
| A.D. 1969 | Neil Armstrong landed on the Moon |
| **A.D. 1978** | **Mainland China began its economic reform** |
| A.D. 1989 | Communists lost control of most eastern European countries |

# Did You Know?

**... that rules of business practice have been in place in China for 2,300 years?**

Many Chinese regarded Fàn Lì, a minister who lived in the Warring States, as the patron saint of merchants. Fàn, also known as Táo Zhūgōng, retired from politics after assisting his emperor to destroy the State of Wú. He became a merchant and was said to have become fabulously wealthy by practising certain rules in business. These rules covered all aspects of business from customer service to inflation, and were adopted by many Chinese business people. You will find a complete list of his business principles in Chapter 13.

**... that it was a merchant who put China's First Emperor Shǐ Huángdì on the throne?**

Though born into a royal family in the State of Qín, Shǐ Huángdì was in exile when he was young. A merchant called Lǚ Bùwéi found him and discovered the boy's relationship with the king of Qín. He saw the boy as "an extremely rare commodity" and invested heavily to engineer the return of Shǐ Huángdì to Qín's throne. He eventually succeeded, became Prime Minister of Qín, and supervised the writing of what amounted to an encyclopedia of the time, *Lǚ Shì Chūn Qiu*.

**... that the Great Wall of China was NOT the most costly building project by** Shǐ Huángdì?

Though the Great Wall is the only man-made object visible from outer space, it was not the most expensive building project carried out by Shǐ Huángdì. His most extravagant project was the construction of his palaces and tomb, which might have employed 1.5 million people at one time. In comparison, building the Great Wall only used 300,000 people.

**... that paper was NOT invented for the purpose of writing?**

Paper was invented in A.D. 105 in China, by a man called Cài Lún. The first form of paper used hemp plant or tree bark for fibre, and was too coarse for writing. It was used for wrapping things. Later the art was refined and paper was used for writing. Prior to paper, Chinese carved their writings on bones during the Shāng Dynasty and later on bamboo strips during the Zhōu and Qín dynasties.

**... that the first seismograph was developed almost 2,000 years ago in China?**

The first seismograph was developed by a man called Zhāng Héng (A.D. 78-139). Besides seismography, he also studied natural phenomena. He denied that disasters were caused by the gods' anger. He theorized that the earth is like the yoke of an egg, and determined the positions of the equator, the ecliptic, and the polar stars. He discovered that the moon rotates around the earth, and that it receives light from the sun. From there he correctly explained the phenomenon of wax and wane, and that it is the earth's shadow that causes a lunar eclipse.

## ... that woodblock printing was used in China 500 years before the Gutenberg press?

Printing was invented in China around the tenth century. Some attributed the invention to a high official in Sìchuān (Szechwen) who ordered the printing of *Anthology of Literature* from woodblocks. Others thought it was Féng Tāo, a prime minister of the time, who printed *The Nine Classics* from woodblocks in A.D. 953. Printing was used extensively during the later Sòng Dynasty.

## ... that the first paper bank note was issued in China in 1024?

Development of paper bank notes did not happen overnight. By the ninth century, the merchants in China had already developed a money-draft system to supplement the often short supply of metal currency. Later private banks began to issue certificates of deposits. In 1024, the government created the world's first national banknotes. Thus nearly 1,000 years ago, China already had an efficient currency system.

Central District of Hong Kong. The tall building in the background is the Bank of China.
(Photo courtesy of David Au)

# Chapter Two

# *H*ong Kong, Taiwan and Mainland China

Most of the Chinese people in North America came from either Hong Kong, Taiwan or mainland China. Although all three places are populated by Chinese, they are under three different governments. Since each government provides a different environment for its people, your customers from these three areas will likely have different experiences and expectations. This chapter will give an overview of the history, economic policies and way of life in these three areas. Understanding your customers' homeland and history can help you understand their world view.

## *Origin of the three governments*

Before the mid-1800's, Hong Kong, Taiwan and mainland China were all under the Qing government. At that time, Hong Kong was a barren island frequented by fishermen and pirates, while Taiwan was inhabited by aborigines and settlers from the mainland. China herself was showing signs of decline after years of internal unrest and widespread corruption.

The nineteenth century was a time of European colonial expansion, trading and greed. The Europeans imported a huge amount of silk and tea from China, but for a while they could not

31

find a commodity the Chinese needed. To help balance the trade deficit, Britain began smuggling opium into China. Millions of Chinese became opium addicts. China suffered from a huge out-flow of silver to pay for the drug, which seriously disturbed the economy. In 1839, the Chinese government stopped the illegal trade and confiscated more than 20,000 chests of opium. Britain sent in the navy in response, and started the Opium War. Britain won, and China was forced to sign the Treaty of Nánjīng in 1842. Part of the treaty required China to give Hong Kong to Britain. That was the beginning of British rule in Hong Kong.

After the Treaty of Nánjīng, almost every foreign power wanted a piece of China. Over the next few decades, China had to sign more treaties with the West, each time giving away more territories and rights. In 1894, China lost a war to Japan over control of Korea, and had to give Taiwan away to Japan. Taiwan remained under Japanese rule until the end of the Second World War.

The Revolution in 1911, under Dr. Sun Yat-sen, put an end to the Qīng Dynasty, but the country broke up into civil war almost immediately. In 1928, the Nationalists, under Chiang Kai-shek, re-united China again. Yet in spite of unity, the Nationalists still had two formidable problems — increasing Japanese aggression and Communist opposition.

In 1937, Japan invaded China. Millions of people were killed. The war with Japan lasted until 1945, when Japan surrendered to the Allies. Taiwan was returned to Chinese rule. In the mean-time, led by Máo Zédōng, the Communist forces grew.

By 1949, the Communists had control of the entire mainland, and the People's Republic of China (PRC) was formed. The

Nationalists retreated to Taiwan. Since then, Taiwan has been under Nationalist rule.

Thus since 1949, what used to be China was divided into three separate states: the British colonial state in Hong Kong, the Nationalist state in Taiwan, and the Socialist state on the mainland. For almost thirty years, the three states followed different economic policies. By the late seventies, the PRC began a series of economic reforms after years of economic stagnation. At the same time, both Hong Kong and Taiwan were experiencing a shortage of labour and stiff competition from developing countries. Out of economic necessity, fuelled by a sense of patriotism, the people in the three areas began to cooperate. While the PRC provides an inexpensive labour force and other resources, Hong Kong and Taiwan provide the much-needed capital and business skills. The complementary relationship has benefited everybody in the Chinese trio. All three areas have enjoyed growth at a rate they have not seen in years.

While the living standards in all three areas have shown dramatic improvements since the cooperation began, most people in Hong Kong and Taiwan are concerned about their political future. In a Joint Declaration in 1984, Britain agreed to return Hong Kong to China by 1997. The future of Taiwan, however, is still uncertain. The anticipated change and uncertainties have caused much anxiety in these areas. Many have left or want to leave their homelands to settle into a more stable environment. Canada, with its stable political system and multicultural policy, is a country of preferred choice.

## Figure 2.1: Chinese People in Mainland China, Taiwan, Hong Kong and Southeast Asia

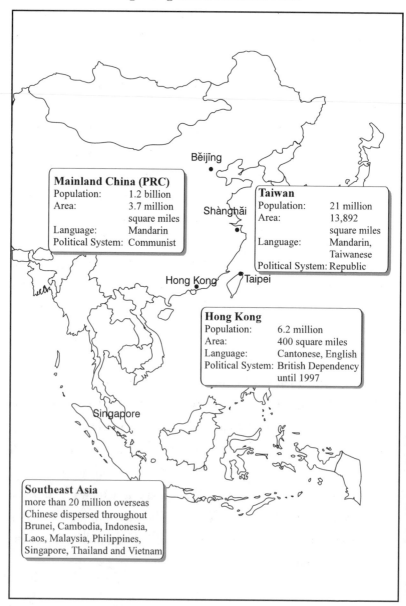

Běijīng

**Mainland China (PRC)**
Population:          1.2 billion
Area:               3.7 million
                    square miles
Language:           Mandarin
Political System:   Communist

Shànghǎi

**Taiwan**
Population:          21 million
Area:               13,892
                    square miles
Language:           Mandarin,
                    Taiwanese
Political System: Republic

Hong Kong          Taipei

**Hong Kong**
Population:          6.2 million
Area:               400 square miles
Language:           Cantonese, English
Political System: British Dependency
                    until 1997

Singapore

**Southeast Asia**
more than 20 million overseas
Chinese dispersed throughout
Brunei, Cambodia, Indonesia,
Laos, Malaysia, Philippines,
Singapore, Thailand and Vietnam

## *Hong Kong*

### Key Facts

| | |
|---|---|
| Population | 6.2 million |
| Area | 400 sq. miles (1,045 sq. km) |
| Official languages | Chinese, English |
| Spoken dialect | Cantonese |
| Political system | British Dependency |

### The land and its past

Hong Kong is located on the southern coast of China. Geographically, it comprises of a part of the mainland and more than 235 islands, with a total land area of about 400 square miles (1,045 sq. km). The mainland part has two sections: the Kowloon Peninsula in the south, and the New Territories in the north. The main island, Hong Kong Island, lies about a mile south of Kowloon Peninsula. Most commercial activities take place along the northern coast of Hong Kong Island and in the Kowloon Peninsula.

The Hong Kong Island itself has been under British rule since 1842. The Kowloon Peninsula was given to Britain in 1860. The rest of Hong Kong was leased to Britain for 99 years in 1898. This lease will expire in 1997, and Britain has agreed to return the entire Hong Kong to China on July 1 of that year.

### The people and their livelihood

Devoid of natural resources, Hong Kong's scant 400 square miles of land has to support a population of 6.2 million people. This means there are over 15,000 people for every square mile of land, making Hong Kong one of the most densely populated places in the world. In comparison, Metropolitan Toronto has an area of 2,156 square miles, 3.89 million people, or 1,800 people per square mile; Greater Vancouver has an area of 1,077 square miles and a population of 1.78 million, or less than 1,700 people per square mile.

Compounding the problem is Hong Kong's topography. The vast part of Hong Kong is mountainous and uninhabitable, limiting most people and activities to the much smaller commercial and residential areas. The density of the Hong Kong Island and Kowloon Peninsula, for example, is 67,132 people per square mile.

Yet the limited space and resources have not discouraged Hong Kong people from doing well. Over the past two decades, the Hong Kong economy has more than quadrupled in size. Its Gross Domestic Product (GDP) per capita (1994) is U.S.$21,800, surpassing that of the United Kingdom, Canada and Australia. Today, it is the fourth largest banking centre and the eighth largest trading entity in the world. Over 100 banks and 4 stock exchanges are in Hong Kong. Its unemployment rate was a mere 2.1% in 1994 and around 3% in 1995. Table 2.1 shows some of Hong Kong's economic and social indicators.[1]

Hong Kong owes much of its success to its hardworking and entrepreneurial people, its strategic location and the laissez-faire philosophy of the government. Ingenuity of the people is evident everywhere. For example, to make more living space, Hong Kong has literally flattened mountains and reclaimed dry land from the sea. To enable so many people to move around such a small area without undue congestion, Hong Kong has developed an extremely efficient transit system. During the Korean War, when the United Nations imposed an embargo on trade with China, Hong Kong turned itself into a manufacturing centre. After 1978, when China began to reform its economy, Hong Kong once again changed its role and became a service centre. The scarcity of resources and the constant change in the environment have made the Hong Kong people highly adaptive, efficient and competitive.

## Living in Hong Kong

It is not too difficult to imagine the effect of the dense population and everyday competition on people's behaviour. Anthropologists have identified a culture typical of societies where there

### Table 2.1
### Hong Kong Economic and Social Indicators (1994)

| | | |
|---|---|---|
| GDP per capita | | U.S. $21,760 |
| Hang Seng Index (1994 year high) | | 12,599 |
| Government budget | | U.S. $21 billion |
| Cargo throughput | port | 141 million tonnes |
| | airport | 1.29 million tonnes |
| Number of workers | manufacturing | 446,000 |
| | service | 2.21 million |
| Unemployment rate | | 2.1% |
| Tourists | | 9.3 million |
| Trips taken abroad | | 32.6 million |
| Telephone lines per 1000 people | | 506 |
| Fax lines per 1000 people | | 41 |
| Outward international telephone traffic | | 1,304 million min. |

is a division of labour, a free market and a huge number of people living in proximity. They call such a culture the Industrial-Commercial-Urban, or the ICU (no pun intended) culture. Some places with an ICU culture are Los Angeles, New York and Hong Kong. People who live in an ICU culture generally have a faster pace of life. This is especially true of Hong Kong. In a recent study, social psychologist Robert Levine compared the pace of life in six societies, using walking speed, accuracy of bank clocks, and promptness of financial transactions as criteria. He found Hong Kong to be fastest, even ahead of Japan.[2] People accustomed to a slower pace of life may find some behaviours of people from ICU cultures to be abrupt and impersonal.

Most people in Hong Kong live in concrete highrise apartments which are called flats. Typically, the highrises are built in clusters, often on top of shopping outlets. Many of these flats are small and are very expensive by Canadian standards. For example, it is common to find an apartment with three bedrooms, a living room, a kitchen and a bathroom, all fitting into a space of 800 square feet, and selling for half a million U.S. dollars. For security reasons, most people install a gate with metal bars outside their own apartment doors. Very few people live in single-family homes because of the high land cost.

Partly due to the lack of space and partly for convenience, the people in Hong Kong eat out a lot, especially when they are entertaining guests. A good restaurant may see its customers lined up for more than an hour before they can be seated. Whether at home or eating out, Hong Kong people eat a lot of rice, vegetables, seafood, pork and poultry.

Besides the sheer number of people, Canadian visitors to Hong Kong are often overwhelmed by two things about its environment: the high level of background noise and the hot, humid weather. There are a number of factors contributing to the high level of background noise in Hong Kong. In the first place, the streets are filled with pedestrians. In spite of the efficient roadways and transit system, traffic is always heavy. Construction is going on everywhere. The combined effect is a very high level of background noise, at times audible from 10 or 20 storeys above. Often people must speak loudly to be heard.

Hong Kong has a semi-tropical climate. Its summer temperature can reach to 35°C (95°F) or more, and is very humid. As a result, mildew and insects are common in certain areas. Many people store their clothing in chests and use moth-balls to keep the insects away.

The city of Hong Kong is a very special place. It sees cutting-edge technology running side by side with ancient traditions. It sees a highly competitive people living in a culture that values harmony. It is a place where every square inch of land and every minute of time is put to use. It is a place with a lot of people and very little resources, but through ingenuity and hard work, the people have prospered through good times and bad.

## Your customers from Hong Kong

We all carry a piece of the past into the present. Your customers from Hong Kong are no exception. It is likely they are still used to the very fast-paced culture characteristic of Hong Kong. Your ability to provide efficient service can earn you a lot of respect. At the same time, as newcomers to this country, many will need more information on local products and services. Your best strategy is to be both efficient and personable. This means you must have excellent product knowledge, be responsive to your customers' needs and be friendly.

Most people from Hong Kong, especially the younger generation, speak English as their second language. People of the older generation may or may not understand English. If you find it difficult to communicate with your customers because their English is not as fluent as yours, refer to Part III of this book on how to communicate across a language difference.

## *Taiwan*

### Key facts

| | |
|---|---|
| Population | 21 million |
| Area | 13,892 square miles (35,980 sq.km) |
| Official language | Mandarin (also called *Guoyu* in Taiwan) |
| Spoken dialects | Mandarin, Taiwanese, Fujianese |
| Political system | Republic |
| Capital | Taipei |

### The land and its past

Taiwan is an island off the Chinese coast, about 90 miles away from the mainland. It is slightly larger than Vancouver Island in British Columbia, and is more than six times the area of Prince Edward Island. Most parts of the island are mountainous. The capital, Taipei, is located at the northern end.

Except for some aborigines, few people lived on the island before the seventeenth century. Some Portuguese sailors landed there in 1590 and named it Formosa, the Beautiful Island. In mid-seventeenth century, some Dutch traders occupied a Taiwanese port. They were later driven out by a Míng general, Koxinga, who occupied the island as a stronghold against the Manchu government during the early part of the Qīng Dynasty. In 1683, the Manchu government conquered the island.

Japan controlled Taiwan between 1895 and 1945. Some of the Japanese buildings and influences are still visible in many parts of the island. Taiwan returned to Chinese rule after Japan surrendered at the end of the Second World War.

In 1949, after their defeat by Máo Zédōng's Communist forces, the Chinese Nationalist government retreated to Taiwan. Since then, both governments have maintained their respective claims to Taiwan as a province of China, and each claims to be the legal ruler of the entire China. Tension remains high between the two governments.

In the late eighties, while the PRC was undergoing economic reform, Taiwan also went through a political reform. The martial law that had been enforced for 38 years was lifted, and increasing democracy was allowed. Gradually, the tension between Taiwan and the mainland began to ease off. Taiwan allowed its citizens to visit the mainland. Indirect flights and business cooperation were permitted.

Since the beginning of 1995, however, the tension between the two sides has tightened up again. The mainland government

A corner of Taipei.
(Photo courtesy of Taipei Economic & Cultural Office)

expressed its disappointment over Taiwanese President Lee Teng-hui's unofficial visit to the United States and other countries, and raised concerns about Taiwan's first election and its political future. The PRC conducted a number of military exercises in the surrounding areas, including the use of missiles. The exercises caused a great deal of concern to the people in Taiwan.

## People and their livelihood

There are 21 million people living on the island, or a density of 1,512 persons per square mile. In comparison, Canada has 28 million people and an area of 3.8 million square miles, or a density of 7 persons per square mile. Almost all the people of Taiwan live along the coastal plain on the western side of the island. Three-quarters of the people live in urban areas, especially in Taipei and Kaohsiung.

Most of Taiwan's economy relies heavily on manufacturing and foreign trade. Its products range from electronics to plastics, and its trade is with the United States, Japan, Hong Kong and Europe. Taiwan also has a significant amount of agricultural and forest products, as well as a respectable fishing industry. Taiwan has a good network of roads, railroads, and an excellent transit system. Automobiles are very expensive because of tax. On average, there is only one automobile for every 30 people.

The Nationalist government pursues a very aggressive economic development program. In 1965, it stopped receiving economic aid from the USA. Since then, the economy not only stood on its own, but flourished. The past decades of economic stability in the island have produced many wealthy industrialists, traders and farmers.

## Living in Taiwan

In general, life in Taiwan is less hurried than in Hong Kong. However, the people of Taiwan still enjoy prompt services and financial transactions. Public transit is on schedule. Both Taipei and Kaohsiung are large cities with world-class facilities.

Taipei, the capital, is linked to all parts of the island by roads and rails, and is also a commercial, cultural and tourist centre. Some of its famous landmarks include the Grand Hotel which resembles a Chinese palace, the Lungshan Temple which sees thousands of Buddhist admirers a day, the National Palace Museum and the Chiang Kai-shek Memorial Hall. Taipei has a population of 2.6 million, or 25,000 persons per square mile. Overcrowded housing, traffic and air pollution are just some of the chronic problems in the city. Outside Taipei, many people live along the coastal plain on the western side of the island, especially near Kaohsiung. Kaohsiung is a port and a manufacturing centre. Many smaller cities along the western coast are also industrialized.

About 20% of the people in Taiwan are farmers. A typical farm in Taiwan is two or three acres, very small by North American standards. Many of these small farms are located on terraced hillsides. Yet the farmers in Taiwan live very well by Asian standards. Fields are generally tilled with power tillers instead of buffaloes. Farmhouses are made of brick, with tiled roofs and a central courtyard, and are often equipped with modern electronics. Using fertilizers, Taiwanese farmers enjoy two or three crops a year from the same field.

## Your customers from Taiwan

Over the past few years, an increasing number of people are coming from Taiwan. It is expected that this trend will continue in the near future. Many of these newcomers are business immigrants. For example, although Taiwan ranks fourth or fifth as a source country for new immigrants over the past five years, it ranks second as a source country for business immigrants after Hong Kong.[3]

Customers from Taiwan generally follow the Chinese traditions closely. Most of them are used to urban living and modern technology. Like all newcomers, many will require information about local products, services and business practices. To provide a personable service consistent with Chinese traditions and communication style will be the key to success in serving customers from Taiwan. The ability to develop a long term business relationship with them is a definite advantage.

Although an increasing number of people in Taiwan can speak English, the language is still not commonly used. However a number of people from Taiwan have either studied or done business in North America before, and are fluent in English. Many parents are also sending their children to Canada to learn English.

## *Mainland China*

### Key Facts

| | |
|---|---|
| Population | 1.2 billion |
| Area | 3.696 million square miles (9.572 million sq.km) |

| | |
|---|---|
| Official language | Mandarin (also called *Pǔtōnghuà* in China) |
| Spoken dialects | Over 100 dialects |
| Political system | Communist |
| Capital | Běijing |

## The land and its recent past

China is the world's third largest country in area, next to Russia and Canada. It takes up one fifth of Asia. It has some of the highest mountains and most fertile farmlands in the world. Most people, cities and farmlands are located in the eastern third of the country.

Shortly after the People's Republic was established in 1949, the Communist government redistributed land among the peasants and established strong control over China. From 1953 to 1957, during the First Five-Year Plan, all important industries were brought under government control, while peasants' landholdings were combined into cooperatives. In 1958, China began its Second Five-Year Plan, better known as The Great Leap Forward. Workers were asked to work long shifts while agricultural cooperatives were combined into huge communes. The intent was to increase production dramatically. The result, however, was a near economic disaster. Meanwhile, the Communist Party was divided into two factions, the idealists and the pragmatists.

In 1966, Máo Zédōng rallied the young people to support the idealists. The young people, calling themselves the Red Guard, seized control of many provincial and municipal governments. Both the government and the economy were brought to a standstill. In 1967, the government called in the army to restore order in the country. After Máo's death in 1976, some of the extreme idealists were imprisoned. The pragmatists, first led by Huá Guófēng and later by Dèng Xiǎopíng, came to power.

In 1978, China began its economic reform. The government began to free up the markets gradually. Peasants were allowed to keep or trade a good part of their produce. Foreign trading was encouraged and foreign capital and technologies were welcome. The government even designated five Special Economic Zones (SEZ) and a number of "open areas" for foreign involvement. The result of this reform was immediate and dramatic. Production of all crops grew at an unprecedented rate. Capital poured into China by tens of millions of dollars, mostly from Hong Kong and Taiwan. Small enterprises, from factories to restaurants, sprang up like mushrooms. Some areas, such as Shēnzhèn, changed from a small town to a metropolitan city within a few short years.

After almost two decades of economic reform, China has changed dramatically. The reform not only raised most people's living standards, it also produced many wealthy entrepreneurs.

## People and their livelihood

China is the most populous country in the world. One in every five people on the planet lives in China. Ninety percent of the 1.2 billion people live in the eastern half of the country. Seventy-four percent of the people live in rural areas. Even though only about a quarter of its people live in cities, there are more than 30 cities in China that have a population exceeding 1 million. Among them are:

| Shànghǎi | 8 million |
| Běijīng | 7.5 million |
| Guǎngzhōu (Canton) | 6.2 million |

In terms of total economic production, China has one of the world's largest economies. Its 1992 GDP was an impressive U.S.$434 billion. But when the total production is divided by the number of people, the per capita GDP is low. Moreover, contribution to the GDP is not proportional to the number of workers involved. For example, 60% of all Chinese workers are involved in farming, but agriculture only makes up 24% of the GDP. The approximate breakdown of China's GDP and the percentage of population involved is summarized in Table 2.2.

**Table 2.2**
**PRC Production and Workers by Economic Activities**

|  | *Percent of GDP* | *Percent of Workers* |
|---|---|---|
| Manufacturing and mining | 42% | 17% |
| Agriculture, forestry and fishing | 24% | 60% |
| Services | 34% | 23% |

Economic progress since the 1978 reform has been very impressive. China's GDP grew by 8% a year for 14 years, making China one of the fastest growing economies in the world.[4] Growth in 1994 was a stunning 11.8%. Growth in foreign trade is even more impressive. Table 2.3 compares some foreign trade indicators between 1993 and 1994.

## Table 2.3
## PRC Foreign Trades 1993 and 1994
### in U.S.$billion

|  | 1993 | 1994 |
|---|---|---|
| Exports | 92 | 120 |
| Imports | 105 | 115 |
| Foreign direct investment | 27.5 | 28.8 |
| Foreign exchange reserve | 22.4 | 49 |

In spite of the reform, China's economy today is still not a free market economy. In a way, it is a hybrid between a bureaucratic command system and a market economy. Although central planning is gone, the government still frequently intervenes in enterprise operations. The government owns, controls and operates most important industries, the banking system, transportation and foreign trade. Moreover, most people in China are still employed by the government.

## Living in China

City life in China is very different from life in the countryside. Generally, city residents enjoy higher wages and have more cultural activities than rural people.

In the cities, most people either live in older neighbourhoods or in apartment complexes built by the government or their employers. Unlike Canada, people in China usually cannot choose the apartment they like. Instead, apartments are assigned to them by the unit, or *Dānwèi*, for which they work. Sometimes, where there is a housing shortage, two families may be required to share

Modern buildings in a historical city — Běijīng today.
(Photo courtesy of Mathew Leung)

an apartment. Each apartment complex elects its own residents' committee to supervise the neighbourhood facilities and programs.

City residents generally have a higher income than rural people, but their income is still low by Western standards. On the other hand, most households have at least two wage earners. Both rent and food costs are very low, as is medical care, child care and most forms of recreation. Generally, each household can afford one or two bicycles, a television and some appliances.

In the rural areas, people live in a system of collective ownership. Each unit in the system is called a collective. In the past, a collective planned and controlled all economic activities of the villages under its jurisdiction. Since 1979, collectives merely set up production contracts with individual families. As long as the families meet the terms of the contract, they are allowed to keep the remainder of their production. Families are also allowed to sell a service to the community or manufacture other products instead of doing agricultural work. In such cases, after paying an agreed amount to the collective, they can keep the rest of their proceeds. They are even allowed to hire employees.

The discrepancies in earnings and privileges between cities and the rural areas caused many people to leave the countryside to seek jobs in the cities. Unfortunately, many of these job-seekers are not skilled and are ill-equipped for city living. Failing to find a job but unwilling or unable to return home, they gather around the train stations and become a "floating people." Sometimes they become victims of crime.

## Your customers from mainland China

Most people from mainland China came to Canada as family class or independent immigrants. A small number came here as refugees in the wake of the 1989 Tiānānmén incident. Investors and entrepreneurs, though still small in numbers, have risen from 1.43% in 1994 to 2.52% in the first 8 months of 1995. As family class immigrants, they were sponsored by a close member of their family who is a Canadian, and who agreed to support them while they settle in Canada. As independents, they were selected according to their ability to successfully establish in Canada and contribute positively to the Canadian economy. For those who came as refugees, many were once students who sought Canada's protection after the Chinese government cracked down on pro-democracy student demonstrators in 1989.

People from mainland China arrive in Canada with different amounts of wealth. Some were entrepreneurs or industrialists in China, and may be very wealthy. They usually like to keep a low profile. Some may be students who are working hard to earn a decent living for themselves. Many are very well educated, often with professional degrees, but lacking in Canadian experience or local qualifications. Many of them speak excellent English.

Due to their diversity, there is no set formula for serving the customers from China. Some are very price-conscious, others are more concerned about quality. As China is gradually turning into a consumer society, many Chinese now have very good product knowledge of Western merchandise.

## A Short Trip to Asia

In 1994, I took a trip to Asia to visit my folks in Hong Kong, and to get a glimpse of mainland China and Taiwan. The following are excerpts from my diary.

### March 12, 1994

I could feel Hong Kong the moment the plane arrived, the heat, the humidity, the noise, the change of rhythm. Even my heart beat louder and faster. Visiting Hong Kong is an experience of total involvement.

You cannot possibly feel detached in Hong Kong. Like sitting on a roller-coaster, both your mind and body will be carried by the dynamics of the vehicle. Suddenly you will walk faster, think faster, talk faster. And don't ask the philosophical question of "why in such a hurry." One just doesn't drive at 5 km per hour on the Trans-Canada Highway.

Ten blocks of driving, hundreds of signs, thousands of cars and tens of thousands of pedestrians later, I was back at my dad's apartment. Dad opened the door. It has been two years since I last visited him. He hasn't changed much, but Hong Kong has.

### March 19, 1994

Half of the people I visited this week were talking about immigrating to Canada or Australia. It seemed they knew more about Canada than I knew about Hong Kong. They talked about

The "Long Corridor" in Empress Dowager Cíxǐ's Summer Palace.
A favourite tourist spot in Běijīng.
(Photo courtesy of Mathew Leung)

shopping at the Aberdeen Centre in Richmond, about Yonge Street in Toronto, about Markham and the change that has taken place there over the last ten years.

Alan, a physician friend of mine since our high school years, talked about the house he has in Vancouver's lovely neighbourhood of Kerrisdale. Alan is a typical "astronaut." They use the term to describe someone who travels frequently between Canada and Hong Kong. Alan's family has already made Canada their home, but Alan himself needs to stay and work in Hong Kong.

Linda, another friend, talked about her recent trip to Toronto, her third in two years. She had bought a couple of condominiums in Toronto during the early 90's and saw their values tumble. That did not deter her from visiting the place, or from her plan to immigrate. She said her application is in good progress and she will have an interview next week. If everything goes well, she will be in Toronto by July, this time for good. Linda is not worried about getting a job. She is a secretary.

## March 21, 1994

I took the train to Guǎngzhōu this morning to see a piece of China, something I missed on my last visit. Along the way, I saw both the expected and the unexpected. I expected to see plenty of rice fields and farmers. I did not expect to see highrises in what used to be small towns. The change in China was simply phenomenal.

Guǎngzhōu was congested as usual. From the train station to the hotel, the streets were packed with vehicles and pedestrians. There were a lot of bicycles. The tourist guide told us that for many people in China, a bicycle is their most treasured possession. Along the way, I saw many people wearing simple clothes, carrying a thermos and a small hand-held radio, and riding a bicycle. Austere by Western standards, but I didn't see any signs of poverty.

The hotel was first-class in terms of architectural design and luxury. It stands in sharp contrast with the simple living I saw all around the area. There was a small gift shop and two restaurants. Talking to the hotel manager, I learned that both the hotel and the restaurants were privately owned, by a local Chinese entrepreneur who started off as a street peddler. The manager also told me the owner was away at the time visiting his family in Vancouver, Canada.

## March 25, 1994

I made a point of stopping in Taipei before returning home to Canada. Years ago, visiting the PRC and Taiwan in the same trip was almost unthinkable. The tourist company had arranged a driver to take a few Caucasians and me to our hotel. The driver greeted me in Mandarin, then addressed the rest of the group in English. Outside the terminal, he met a couple of Japanese tourists, and responded to their questions in Japanese.

The short trip through the city took just as much time as the long ride from the airport. Taipei was congested like Guǎngzhōu, except there were a lot more motorcycles. Part of the congestion was caused by the lack of traffic lights in many intersections. There were people everywhere.

After checking into the hotel, I walked to the Central Station for lunch. There in the station were small food bars of every kind, serving a wide variety of the most delicious Taiwanese dishes. Outside the station were numerous street peddlers, selling anything from Chinese carvings to teapots. I stopped by a fortune-teller and asked him what he thought would happen to Taiwan in the coming years. The fortune-teller stared at me for a minute, and said, "If I could predict the future of a nation, I won't be sitting here to predict your future for just a couple of dollars. Why do you want to know anyway? Just live your life and let heavenly order take its course."

[1] *Hong Kong 1995*. Hong Kong Government Information Services.

[2] Bond, Michael Harris. *Beyond the Chinese Face - Insights from Psychology*. Oxford University Press, 1991, p.49.

[3] *Facts and Figures: Overview of Immigration*. Citizenship and Immigration Canada, November 1994.

[4] Perkins, Dwight. "Completing China's Move to the Market." *Journal of Economic Perspective*, Vol 8(2), Spring, 1994, p.24.

A new citizen celebrates Canada Day.
(Photo courtesy of S.U.C.C.E.S.S.)

# Chapter Three

# *𝒯*he Challenges
# of Starting a New Life

All of us have gone through change sometime in our lives. We generally think of it as putting an end to some parts of ourselves in order to have a new beginning. In reality, in between the ending and the new beginning is a transitory period when we have decided to start something new but have not completely let go of the past. Psychologists tell us that this transitory phase is both natural and necessary.

Settling into a new country is a major change in every immigrant's life. They all go through a transitory period of adjustment after they arrive. During this period, a newcomer may adjust certain of his expectations and behaviours in order to function in the new culture. According to psychologist John W. Berry, such an adjustment may result in one of these four outcomes:[1]

- Assimilation: the newcomer gives up his heritage culture to adopt the host culture.
- Integration: the newcomer retains his heritage and takes on the host culture.
- Separation: the newcomer retains his heritage culture and does not move into the host culture.
- Marginalization: the newcomer remains apart from both the

host and heritage cultures.

Of these four outcomes, integration is desired by most immigrants. It is also the intended outcome of Canada's multicultural policy. Suppliers should note that newcomers do not have to give up their own culture in order to integrate.

Depending on the person, the process of integration may take from a few months to a few years, usually in five stages. This chapter describes how a new immigrant feels when he is going through each stage, what his consumer needs are, the way he sees the commercial world, and how one can provide responsive service to meet his needs.

People who interact with new immigrants should have a basic understanding of this integration process and the five stages it comprises. They should recognize that their customers' needs and concerns will change as they pass from one stage to another. Sometimes new immigrants may even do things differently from the way they normally do while they are adjusting to their new lives. For example, they may take a longer time to make a "simple decision." To those who are less familiar with integration, some of these behaviours may appear negative. Unfortunately, sometimes people mistakenly associate these transitory behaviours with the immigrant's cultural or ethnic origin, leading to unnecessary and incorrect stereotyping.

## *Before moving to Canada*

The challenges facing new immigrants begin long before they land in Canada. The moment they begin entertaining the idea of emigrating, they put themselves on a rollercoaster of hope and despair, dilemma and decisions, joy and frustration. Most Chinese immigrants who came to Canada over the last few years were well established in their homelands. Either they were very well employed, or were running a successful business. To uproot everything in the prime of their lives and move to unfamiliar territory takes a lot of courage and careful planning. Overcoming the fear of uncertainty was probably their first major challenge.

Once they decided to make the move, they faced more challenges. In a number of cases, not everyone in the family supports the decision. For example, opposition may come from the applicants' parents, who may not want to move. Even when the parents support the move, they may not be able to meet the immigration criteria. Applicants often have to make a choice between severing a part of their extended family or not making the move at all. Those who understand the strong family ties in Asian culture will appreciate the difficulty of this dilemma.

Filing the application is the beginning of a long, and often trying, waiting period. This is the time when one is tuned into all the bad news about the new country. The applicant often hears news about how difficult it is to find a job in Canada; about the anti-immigrant sentiment; about those not able to make the adjustment and had to return home, only to find that they are no longer able to buy back the kind of accommodation they used to live in because of inflation. The waiting period ends with an interview and an official approval. Initially, most feel very excited by the acceptance. This could be followed by a number of nerve-wracking events such as resigning from their positions, selling or renting out their homes, shopping and packing, saying farewell to friends and relatives and coming to consensus over matters affecting the family.

Some Canadian marketers and suppliers start to build their relationship with their customers at this early stage of their customers' move. Many have been very successful. If you are thinking of starting a relationship with your customers at this stage, you may consider forming an alliance with some immigration consultants. This is especially useful if you are in real estate or investment brokerage. Your customers at this stage are likely looking for information to help them overcome their feeling of uncertainty. They also need someone whom they can count on after they move to Canada. If you have a good reputation as a reliable supplier who cares for the customers, you will find them very receptive to starting a business relationship with you at this stage.

## The five stages of social adjustment

The period of social adjustment begins the day your customers land in Canada. In general, there are five stages. The intensity of emotion and duration of each stage vary from individual to individual, depending on one's personality, age and former exposure to Western culture. The five stages are:

1. Excitement
2. Initial cultural shock
3. Superficial adjustment
4. Depression
5. Acceptance of host culture

## Excitement

This is the honeymoon period for people going through positive change. Most immigrants report feelings of elation after they arrive. They are impressed by the fresher quality of the air, the general cleanliness of the city, the spaciousness of the houses, the size of the supermarkets and the general polite behaviour of the people. They like seeing the birds and small animals which they never saw in a large metropolitan setting. They like the fact that they can return merchandise within a certain period of time after the purchase. Generally, they feel like tourists on vacation, seeing new things every day.

## Initial cultural shock

Inevitably, the honeymoon period cannot last forever. Soon they begin to experience the conflict and inconvenience of the new culture. The system is different, the pace is different. Even if they are fluent in English, they still find it difficult to communicate because of accent and expressions. They find their houses too open, and suffer from a general sense of insecurity. Most of them do not have a Canadian driver's licence yet and find it inconvenient to have to get a ride wherever they go. They are not used to the idea that some people can receive U.I. or welfare even though they are not working. Above all, they find it discouraging when employers turn down their job applications due to their lack of local experience.

## Superficial adjustment

After a while, newcomers succeed in learning a few things to cope with the change. For example, they begin to understand the cashiers when they ask: "Do you want a bag?" They have learned to say "hi" to their neighbours, and can use expressions such as "you bet" (an expression which until now they associated only with gambling). By this time, many have learned how to drive and have become more independent. They have come to terms with reality and will consider the possibility of finding work outside their areas of expertise. In general, this is the stage when they begin getting used to their surroundings, the system and the way of life in Canada.

## Depression

Superficial adjustment does not solve some of the deep-rooted problems facing new immigrants. Eventually, they begin to feel the gravity of some of these problems:

- Unable to find a satisfactory job, leading to a loss of self-esteem, lack of security, and a sense of detachment from society.
- General feeling of dissatisfaction caused by daily frustrations, such as the first encounter with black ice, the rain that lasts for days on end, and the long line-ups in banks and other places.
- Difficulty socializing with Canadians as they cannot find a suitable common subject of conversation besides the weather.
- General dissatisfaction with the system, such as the high taxes and insurance costs, and a perceived lack of discipline in most public schools.

Their frustration and dissatisfaction often lead to a period of depression. Some return to their source countries during this period.

### Acceptance of host culture

Over time, new immigrants will come out of the depression stage and accept the host culture. This is the time when they come to accept their new role in society. They begin to appreciate the host culture and the Canadian way of life. Only now are the new immigrants fully integrated into the Canadian society.

## A new immigrant's needs

As newcomers go through integration, their consumer needs also change. Psychologist Dr. Abraham Maslow did a lot of studies on needs. He found that human needs have five different levels of urgency. Human beings will always find ways to satisfy the more basic needs before paying attention to the next level of needs. In other words, these five levels of needs form a hierarchy.

On the bottom of this hierarchy are our physical needs, such as our needs for food, shelter and clothing. Some call this level the need for survival. When this level of needs is satisfied, a person will be driven by the next level, which is the need for safety. Above this level is the level of social needs, such as the need to be accepted by others. On top of our social needs is the need for self-esteem, such as having a sense of self-worth and respect from others. The final one is the level of self-actualization. This is the level of need for self-fulfilment. Figure 3.1 illustrates this hierarchy of needs according to Maslow.

This hierarchy of needs is universal, and can be applied to immigrants regardless of cultural origin. In fact, the hierarchy applies to each of the immigrant's spheres of life. According to Sociologist G. Neuwirth, immigrants have five spheres of life:[2]

## Figure 3.1: Hierarchy of Needs According to Abraham Maslow

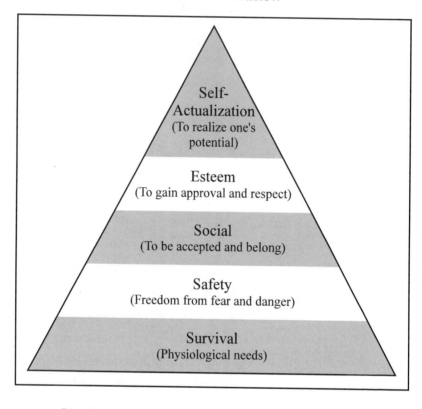

- Physical-mental well-being
- Linguistic
- Economic
- Civic/Social welfare
- Privacy/Sociability

In each sphere of life, immigrants' concerns change as their needs change. For example, when they first arrive, their immediate concerns are generally related to survival. The need for survival is manifested in a number of ways. They will need temporary shelter, which may range from a relative's house to hotel accommodation (physical well-being). If they are not conversant in English, they will need basic interpretation (linguistic). Within the first few days, they will set up bank accounts (economic). They will also find out how to get around by public transit or by car (civic welfare).

Once the immigrants' need for survival is satisfied in a particular sphere of life, they will turn their attention to the next level of needs, namely safety. For example, in the economic sphere, after setting up bank accounts, they may begin looking for work.

Table 3.1 shows how Maslow's hierarchy of needs can be applied to various spheres of life, according to Neuwirth. Note that the various spheres of life are independent from each other. It is possible that an immigrant is trying to satisfy his esteem needs in one sphere of life while struggling to meet his survival needs in another sphere. It is also possible that a new immigrant is already satisfied with many levels of needs the day he arrives. For example, a very wealthy individual who is fluent in English probably will have little concern about basic employment skills or finding an interpreter.

As a supplier or marketer to new immigrants, you will probably be supplying a variety of services or products in one of their spheres of life. Depending on their circumstances, they may be coming to you with different needs and concerns as they go through the adjustment process. Table 3.1 provides some examples of their needs at different stages in different spheres.

## Table 3.1
### Examples of Applications of Maslow's Hierarchy of Needs in Various Spheres of Life

| NEEDS | PHYSICAL / MENTAL WELL-BEING | LINGUISTIC |
|---|---|---|
| SELF-ACTUALIZATION | Realization of one's potential | |
| ESTEEM | • Move up housing needs<br>• Brand name clothing | • English fluency |
| SOCIAL | • Restaurants<br>• Improved furnishing | • Technical (job-related) English<br>• Colloquial English |
| SAFETY | • Home<br>• Physicians<br>• Alarm systems | • Basic English classes |
| SURVIVAL | • Temporary accommodation<br>• Grocery<br>• Public transportation | • Prefer service in Chinese<br>• Bring interpreter along |

## The paradigm of a new immigrant

A person's paradigm is the way he looks at the world, upon which he acts and reacts. People with different paradigms make different decisions over the same issue, because they see things differently. In a way, our paradigm is our roadmap. We all follow our own internal roadmaps when we explore this world.

## Table 3.1
## Examples of Applications of Maslow's Hierarchy of Needs in Various Spheres of Life (cont.)

| ECONOMIC | CIVIC/SOCIAL WELFARE | PRIVACY / SOCIABILITY |
|---|---|---|
| Realization of one's potential | | |
| • Own business<br>• Medium to high risk investments* | • Additional vehicles<br>• Educational upgrade | • Leisure activities |
| • Business start-up<br>• Accreditation of foreign credentials | • Children's educational programs<br>• Automobile | • Social clubs<br>• Trade associations<br>• Family reunion |
| • Insurance<br>• Job-skills improvement<br>• Low-risk investments<br>• Basic tax knowledge | • Driver's licence<br>• Basic civil rights | • Ethnic organizations<br>• Religious organizations |
| • Basic banking<br>• Start-up income | • Television<br>• Newspapers<br>• Magazines<br>• Maps | • Proximity to friends / relatives<br>• Telecommunication |

Relative to individual's risk comfort

A new immigrant sees the world in a way different from one who was born and raised in Canada. He carries a set of values and assumptions to this country. Some of these values and assumptions remain true over time. Others will be modified as he lives and learns. In order to meet the needs of a new immigrant, it will be tremendously advantageous to understand his paradigm. An effective way to understand a customer's paradigm is to listen to his viewpoints and figure out the assumptions upon which they are based. While it is important to understand an immigrant's paradigm, it is equally important not to generalize his views and consider that all immigrants see the world in the same way. For example, while the following statements have been reported by some new immigrants, but they certainly do not represent every immigrant's view:

- The price of most merchandise is negotiable.
- Brand products are generally better than no brand products.
- Certain brands are better than other brands.
- Salespeople are generally not trustworthy.
- Referral of a friend is better than the best-designed advertisement.
- Wood-frame houses are not durable.
- Certain schools in the city are much better schools than others.
- Import cars are better and more prestigious than most American cars.

## Serving new immigrants

A skillful supplier or marketer can always sense and match their customers' needs as they go through a change. He also recognizes that we all interpret the world according to our past experiences. A new immigrant may look at your products or services with some pre-conceived assumptions which may or may not be true. Many of these assumptions are product-specific and were formed long before they entered your place of business. It will be advantageous to find out their assumptions about your products.

## Let's Welcome Mr. Kwong!

I met Mr. Yiu-ming Kwong at a business lunch organized by the Vancouver-based Sunbrite Business Association. After exchanging business cards and some formal greetings, we talked about what we do. Mr. Kwong was very interested in the idea of this book and volunteered to be interviewed. Why not listen in on our conversation, translated from Cantonese? It took place at Mr. Kwong's lovely home in Richmond, B.C.

**Author:** Mr. Kwong, how long have you been in Canada?

**Kwong:** Not long at all, just over a year.

**Author:** Why did you decide to leave Hong Kong?

**Kwong:** For the same reason as everyone else. I want a stable environment to raise my children. With 1997 approaching, I'm not sure what Hong Kong will be like in a few years. I don't think it will be too bad, but I don't want to take a chance.

**Author:** What did you do for a living when you were in Hong Kong?

**Kwong:** I ran a garment factory.

**Author:** Did you close it down before you left?

**Kwong:** No. My brother, who is also my business partner, is running it for me. I still need to go back a couple of times a year. In fact, my brother has been running the factory part, which is in Shēnzhèn, for the past several years. All I did was look after the administrative office in Hong Kong.

| Author: | What was the first thing you bought in Canada? |
|---|---|
| Kwong: | I don't remember, probably a newspaper or a bag of candy (chuckling). But if you mean the first major item, it was this house. |
| Author: | How did you buy this house? |
| Kwong: | Through a realtor, Mr. Lee, who was introduced to us by our immigration consultant. Mr. Lee called us when we were still in Hong Kong. He received us at the airport the day we arrived. We even stayed at his house on our house-hunting trip. |
| Author: | You mean you came here on an earlier trip just to buy a house? |
| Kwong: | Yes, about half a year before we landed. We wanted to be sure we would have a place to stay the day we arrived. Nobody wants to move twice. |
| Author: | How did you like Mr. Lee's service? |
| Kwong: | Excellent. He knew exactly what we were looking for. He found us a very comfortable house close to a good school and a park. The price was right and the builder is reputable. I also checked out the *fēng shuǐ* and it was flawless. The only thing is, we found it a bit too open. It feels as if anybody can come into your yard or climb through your windows. No one actually did, but it just feels that way. They say every house is like that here. I guess it's only a matter of getting used to it. |
| Author: | What did you buy next? |
| Kwong: | A family car. |
| Author: | Who introduced you to the car salesperson? |
| Kwong: | At first, Mr. Lee introduced us to Mr. Wong, but we didn't buy from him. |
| Author: | What was the problem? |
| Kwong: | I just didn't like his style. He was too pushy, talked |

too much, and always seemed to be hiding something from you. Besides, I just don't like American cars.

**Author:** So what did you do?

**Kwong:** One day, I just walked into an import car dealer. A Caucasian salesman named Tom met me at the foyer. It was the most interesting experience. You see, my English is not too good. I only understood half of the things he said because he was talking too fast and using words I didn't really understand. But in the end, I still bought from him.

**Author:** You still bought from him even though you didn't fully understand what he said?

**Kwong:** Well, I know a lot about cars to begin with, not like a house which is so different from a flat in Hong Kong. I doubt if there are too many new things about cars he could have told me. I liked his sincerity and enthusiasm. When he noticed that I wasn't following what he said, he tried to find another way to explain to me without hurting my feelings. And he wasn't pushy.

**Author:** Besides, you like Mercedes.

**Kwong:** Of course! (laughing) The price is so cheap here compared to Hong Kong.

**Author:** Did you feel good about your purchase?

**Kwong:** I felt great. Not only because I liked the car, but because it was the first all-English transaction I ever did without other people's assistance. I gained confidence in my ability to settle down in this country through that purchase.

**Author:** After you settle down, do you plan to open a branch of your business here?

**Kwong:** I suppose I can, but I don't think I will. I don't know the language that well. I don't have the kind of connections I have back home. Besides, why open a factory here where the labour is so expensive and tax so high?

**Author:** So what is your plan?

**Kwong:** This is why I joined the trade association. To look for ideas and meet people.

When I left, Mr. Kwong accompanied me out to the driveway. There he saw a Caucasian neighbour passing by. He waved and said 'hi.'

**Kwong:** I really like the neighbours here. They're all so friendly and helpful. I think this country would be a paradise if it were not so difficult to earn a living. And the schools should be tightened up just a little bit. When you don't make them work hard in schools, they don't work hard when they grow up. Then they'll have to live on welfare.

At that point, we said good-bye to each other and parted.

---

[1] Berry, J.W. "Acculturation as Varieties of Adaptation." In A.M. Padilla, ed., *Acculturation: Theory, Models and Some New Findings*. Boulder, CO: Westview Press, 1980.

[2] Neuwirth, G. *Immigrant Settlement Indicators: A Conceptual Framework*. Ottawa: Employment and Immigration Canada, 1987.

Chinese values are often reflected in *chūn lián*, well-wishes written on red papers and displayed in stores and homes during festivals. (Photo courtesy of Robert Cheng)

# Chapter Four

# *S*ome Fundamental
# Cultural Concepts

Any Canadian or American who has travelled to the mainland China, Taiwan or Hong Kong can witness the very distinct differences between Chinese and North American culture. Such differences are manifested in the way people interact and communicate, and how they look at family, work and society. This chapter examines some of these differences between the two cultures, especially in these three areas:

- Group harmony
- Social relationships
- Communication styles

Recognizing these differences will help you understand your customers' values and habits, which in turn will make it easier for you to communicate with them and assess their needs. On the other hand, you must never forget that the Chinese community is a very large and diverse group. While you can use the information in this chapter to interpret some of the things your Chinese customers say or do, you should also remember that not all of them see things the same way.

To a large extent, many of the Chinese cultural behaviours

also apply to the people of Japan, Korea and some countries in Southeast Asia, such as Singapore and Thailand. Some people have attributed these international similarities to the teachings of Confucius, and referred to these countries collectively as Confucian Asia.

## Group harmony

Perhaps the most fundamental difference between the North American and Chinese culture is in the emphasis placed upon individual rights versus group harmony. In the West, society places heavy emphasis on individual rights and personal achievement. People are encouraged to speak up for themselves and be creative. Children are trained to be independent as early in life as possible. Society in general rewards individuals with vision and strong personalities. In contrast, throughout the centuries, Chinese people have always placed supreme emphasis on maintaining harmony in society. Often this implies submitting to group authority and adjusting one's preference in favour of the group will. Asian Studies professor Jan Walls summarized this difference between the two cultures in this way: "While the East focuses on the relationship between individuals, the West focuses on the individuals themselves."

The emphasis on maintaining group harmony has significant impact on the way Chinese people behave in a group setting. In fact, when it comes to what is proper behaviour within a group, the North American culture and the Chinese culture are at two extreme ends of a spectrum.

In North America, where society values freedom and individual

rights, people are encouraged to express their opinions, to be straight talkers, to have open debates, to achieve and sometimes even to "blow your own horn." People are complimented for being sociable, eloquent and charismatic. In conversation, a person tends to reveal information about himself as a way to build up a relationship. He can also disagree with others openly on an issue without jeopardizing his personal relationship with his opponents. Words are often used for the purpose of clarifying issues or simply filling up gaps of silence.

The Chinese, on the other hand, value group harmony above individual views. Individuals often downplay their own ability or efforts in public and speak about group accomplishment instead. They adopt an affective style of communication, and adjust their words to the feelings of the other parties. As much as possible, people will conform to the wishes of the group. Diversity is encouraged only to the extent that it does not disrupt the harmony of the group.

Face is an important tool to maintain group harmony. Causing one to lose face is not only rude but a social taboo. To avoid causing others to lose face, Chinese rarely disagree openly. Instead, they express their disagreement in very subtle ways, such as leaving a gap of silence or suddenly changing the topic. Public display of anger, regardless of the cause, is regarded as a sign of immaturity and lack of civility. Not only do the Chinese go to great lengths to avoid causing others to lose face, they also try to enhance each other's face as much as possible. To do so, they may even flatter others with words which, to Western ears, may sound superfluous.

Modesty is another tool to maintain group harmony in the Chinese culture. It is customary for the person on the receiving end of a flattering comment to deny what was said, although this does not mean he dislikes or disagrees with what was said. The person who initiated the flattery should continue with the praise to show his sincerity. The emphasis upon modesty also means one should not blow his own horn in public. Moreover, until one knows the people in a group very well, it is generally regarded as improper and sometimes arrogant either to speak too much or to speak out of turn. Although no formal protocol exists as to when one can speak out in a group, the accepted practice is to follow seniority either by age in social settings or by position in business settings.

In the initial stages of a relationship, since people are not sure of how others see them or view their opinions, they are often slower in revealing themselves. Instead, they may try to ask some seemingly trivial questions to get a feel of others' backgrounds and interests. If they do not feel they can fit in, the relationship will stay at that stage indefinitely (there is, however, never an official end). Otherwise, a deeper and more personal relationship will develop over time. Chinese people are also more selective in joining a group as they want to be sure they can align with the group's goals and behavioural norms. Those who find it difficult to bridge into a group of Chinese people should not feel alienated. In most cases the barrier is not along ethnic lines or language. They need to understand that, in general, Chinese people need to take a longer time to develop a relationship.

It is interesting to note how people of the two cultures see each other when placed into the same room, such as a classroom on campus or a meeting room in a business setting. Often North Americans may find the Chinese too passive, not explicit, formal and overly courteous. The Chinese people may find their North American counterparts too blunt, arrogant, talkative and egotistic. In reality, the two cultures simply have different styles of group building and group dynamics. Once they accept each other's style, productive relationships can be built very easily.

Many Chinese people are beginning to adjust the ways they interact in a group, especially where North Americans are involved. A lot have adopted a more direct approach when it comes to expressing themselves, and no longer feel inhibited to speak out of turn, or the need to downplay themselves. On the other hand, one may still find them overly courteous in meetings or gatherings, especially during the initial stages of a relationship.

## Social relationships

Traditionally, the Chinese hold a highly structured and hierarchical view of social relationships. Confucius advocated a social structure with five relationships between people: emperor-subject, parent-child, elder sibling-younger sibling, husband-wife and between friends. Confucius saw each of these relationships as unequal but complementary. In each relationship, there is a senior or stronger member who provides protection and care for the junior member. In return, the junior member will pay respect to the senior. Even among friends, a hierarchy is established by age. For this reason, it is common for Chinese to refer to friends as brothers or sisters.

This system of complementary relationships has worked very well in China for centuries. In a society in which stability is valued above equality, the system clearly established the authorities and responsibilities of those in power, and the duties and privileges of those not. In the past, this expectation of reciprocal and complementary obligations helped to stabilize the Chinese society in times of war and peace.

Today, China no longer has an emperor. Parents have become a lot less authoritative. The power distance between senior and junior siblings has been greatly reduced. Husbands are not regarded as superior to wives. Friends may still refer to each other as brothers, although few will truly consider a junior friend as someone who needs protection. The power dimension of Confucius' Five Relationships is much diminished, but the principles of seniority, reciprocity and complementary relationships are still deeply entrenched in the Chinese social conscience.

Not all of Confucius' Five Relationships have everyday significance. To begin with, the relationship between the Emperor and his subjects could hardly have been regarded as a social relationship even in the days when there was an emperor. Three of the relationships are within the family. One is a relationship between friends. Thus on an everyday basis, most Chinese distinguish only three main categories of social relationships: family, associates and strangers. In general, family members are closer to each other than to associates, who in turn are closer than strangers. In other words, the type of social bonds we form with other people depends on our relationship with them. In this respect, there is much similarity between the Chinese and the North

American culture. What is different is in the strength of the social bonds, and the expectations and obligations within each relationship category.

## Family

In North America, the term "family" is a very straightforward concept. It refers to the parents and their children, whether blood-related or adopted. It does not typically include in-laws, uncles or close friends. Within a family, all children are equal in hierarchy regardless of seniority. Once a child reaches adulthood, although a formal relationship still exists, the bonds with his or her parents or other siblings are generally much weakened. Children are rarely expected to contribute to the parents financially when they have grown up.

For the Chinese, the term "family" has a broader and deeper connotation. By this I am not referring to the legal definition of who is to be included into a family. Instead I am referring to the group of people with whom a person forms the type of bond he normally forms only with members of his legal family. For most Chinese, this means not only the parents and the children, but the grandparents, parents' siblings and the siblings' children. Often it may even include close friends and long-time servants to the family. Some people refer to the type of relationship between the members of a family as an affective relationship.

Within a family resources are shared. Members will give what they can without necessarily expecting anything in return from the other members. Parents are responsible for their children and their public behaviour. Children or adults, regardless of age, are expected to respect their parents. Not too long ago, that "respect" often meant absolute obedience. Even though parents no longer have nor desire absolute obedience from their children, the sense of filial piety and parental responsibility is still very much part of the Chinese culture. From a very young age, people are taught to be interdependent and to look out for each other. Siblings are not equal in the Western sense. Elder siblings are often entrusted with the responsibility and authority of caring for the younger ones, and a hierarchy is established according to seniority.

While in the West parents spend most of their time preparing their children to become independent, Chinese parents spend most of their time cementing the bond with and between their children. After children reach adulthood, they are still bonded to the rest of the family emotionally, socially and economically. Young people stay home until married regardless of age, and financially contribute to the household. Even after marriage, the family bond still exists, along with the expectation of respect and care (both financial and otherwise) for the parents. The bond is so strong within a Chinese family that often people cannot conceive of themselves outside of the familial context. For most Chinese, the sense of belonging and responsibility continue to exist even after years of separation from the family.

Very often, a man will live with his parents even after he is married. They live together, dine together and make decisions together. The parents are an integral part of the couple's family, and the couple is an integral part of the parents' family. When the young couple have their own children, the family just grows in size. It is therefore possible for a family to have a number of generations living under the same roof, although such multi-generation families are quickly becoming a rarity.

Thus the Chinese have quite a different concept of family from most North Americans. Not only do they generally include members of other generations, they also include siblings and their children. They are expected to share resources, care for, and look out for each other. This expectation and obligation to the rest of the family does not stop when a child reaches adulthood. One is bonded to the family for life. As Singapore's senior minister Lee Kuan-yew puts it: "Eastern societies believe the individual exists in the context of his family."[1]

The strong and lasting family bond is one of the reasons why many Chinese businesses are family-owned, and why they are run so successfully. The system demands all who belong to the family to be loyal to the family. As such, it assures a dedicated workforce whose self-interest is one and the same as the family's interest.

## Associates

In both cultures, the term "associates" means the category of persons to whom one is connected through common functions or interests. This may include people we meet in school, at work, in clubs and so on. To most North Americans, an associate is simply someone who happens to share a certain aspect of life with them. To many Chinese, however, an associate is also a resource. This is because to the Chinese, a person is not just a collection of functions and skills but also a capability as well as a channel to other people. Thus through one's associates and the associates'

associates, one forms a network of resources. Through it one seeks advice and referrals, and through this network one often gets things done. The relationship between associates is partly affective and partly instrumental, since it is built both on a sense of brotherly concern and mutual benefits. In China, this network of associates is known as *guān xì*, or connections. Those who have done business in China will appreciate the importance of this social network. Among North American Chinese, the significance of *guān xì* is less profound, but it is still alive and well.

Having connections does not imply doing anything illegal, or granting favours to those who do not deserve them. Although it is customary in China to gain access to special privileges through connections, the practice is not common and is not condoned by the Chinese in North America. A way of looking at connections is to see it as a referral network combined with a credit system of favours. The system works in this way:

If Mr. Wong wants to buy a car and needs some information about where to get a good deal, he will ask his associates whether they know anyone who works as a car salesperson. Now if his old-time high school friend Mr. Chan has a friend, Mr. Tang, who sells cars, Chan will likely introduce him to Wong. Chan will be acting on the assumption that friends will not let him down.

If in the end Wong did get a good deal from Tang, Chan would have gained face in the endeavour. He gained face in front of Wong because he has proven to be resourceful (i.e. with good connections), and similarly in front of Tang because he has found him a customer. Both parties now owe Chan a favour. Wong will eventually repay Chan by passing him a good tip when he is in need, and Tang will repay Chan by giving him a gift, taking him for lunch or finding him a customer in his business. These reciprocating favours are usually done out of appreciation rather than obligation.

The reverse is also true if Wong did not get a good deal. He would have doubted the quality of Chan's connections, and Chan would have regarded Tang as not "giving face" to him. In such a case, Wong would probably hint to Chan about his receiving a poor service from his friend. Chan would probably ask Tang some open-ended questions to get a picture of what happened and then hint to him his dissatisfaction. From then on, more than likely he would not refer any other associates to Tang in future.

*Guān xì* is in fact a very efficient system of disseminating information with built-in quality check points. Often it is the most reliable source of information about the quality of service or product a supplier provides. As a supplier or marketer, it is not enough just to be connected to a network of associates. Your goal should be to stay connected to as many networks as possible. To be connected to a network is relatively simple. You only need to share some interest or an aspect of life with an associate. To stay connected will depend on whether you can deliver all that your associates expect. Often this means providing a good price, good service and a good quality product.

It is possible that some Chinese may expect favours from their associates that are outside of their regular professional duties. For example, Mrs. Wong might have met realtor Mrs. Leung in the course of looking for a house, and the two became associates. One day Wong may ask Leung if she could look after her five-year old daughter for an evening. In the North American context, Leung may feel that it is not her job to look after a youngster she has never met, and might feel offended. However, Wong might no longer be seeing Leung as a realtor but more as an associate, and does not feel it improper to ask her for such a favour.

As more Chinese people are exposed to the West, more are now making a distinction between the role of an associate from that of a personal friend. Requests besides or beyond one's professional duties are quickly diminishing. However, suppliers should not be surprised or feel slighted in any way if customers ask you for a favour unrelated to your job. Whether you feel comfortable enough to honour the request is your own decision.

## Strangers

In everyday life, we are in contact with a large number of people with whom the association is transient and is not likely to be repeated. These people may include fellow passengers on a bus, the sales staff in a shop, waitresses, passersby and so on. In general, these people have nothing in common, except that they are temporarily sharing a common facility or involved in the same transaction. This group of people will be referred to as strangers. The relationship between strangers is strictly instrumental.

None of Confucius' Five Relationships deals with strangers. It seems that strangers have no place in one's social circle. The Chinese people do not feel there is a need to greet or talk with them. In cases where a conversation is necessary, such as telling a taxi driver the directions or buying something at a store, the conversation is limited strictly to what is required to achieve the purpose. The lack of cordiality towards strangers does not imply any hostility or harm. It is just not customary to be cordial to strangers.

One of the things many new Chinese immigrants like about North America is the warmth of the people. Many newcomers say they have been greeted by Canadians who barely knew them. They like their smiles and genuine friendliness. As a result, many have adopted a friendly and warm attitude towards other strangers they meet in daily life.

## Communication styles

Anyone who has done translation before will know that when a message is translated word for word, it sometimes loses its original meaning. Built into the meaning of any word in any language is a set of connotations and implications that is specific to that language and culture. Even within a language, the same word used in different contexts can have very different meanings.

Just as the meaning of a word varies with its context, the meaning of a phrase or sentence may also vary with the situation. For example, if a mother asks her six-year old daughter: "Have you had lunch yet?" she is probably trying to find out if her daughter needs nourishment. A young man asking a young lady the same question, at least in the Western culture, is offering an invitation for a date. In the Chinese culture, that question is simply a common greeting around noon time.

Thus, words are not the only component of a message. Other components include body language, expressions, tone and volume, pauses and silence, etc. All of these must be interpreted in context. In this respect, the Chinese and North American cultures are very similar. What is different between the two cultures is the relative weight of the spoken words when compared to other components of a message, and the extent to which the meaning of a message is influenced by its situation.

In an individualistic culture where people are free to speak their minds, communication can be precise and direct without having to worry too much about consequences. Unless a person intends to deceive, he will as a rule say what he means and mean what he says. Where the situation calls for greater sensitivity, euphemism and diplomatic expressions may be used, but the wording of a message still reflects its meaning. Only occasionally will people use unspoken or ambivalent messages.

In a collectivist culture, people spend a lot of energy maintaining group harmony by upkeeping each other's face. A careless word or gesture may be interpreted as an insult in the wrong ears, which may lead to undesirable consequences. Only a few generations ago, such mistakes could even be fatal. Even where consequences are not as drastic, a person stands to lose a lot of face if he has to take back his words. People need to be very careful of what they communicate. This attitude can be summarized in the Chinese saying: "A gentleman will value his promise as if it is worth a thousand pieces of gold."

Communication in a collectivist culture is not only characterized by careful selection of words but by the frequent use of probes, hints and ambivalent or even unspoken messages. This is especially true when it comes to the making of or responding to requests. This is because a person making a request not only needs to be concerned about what he says, but also with the face of his listener. In the Chinese culture, saying "no" to someone's request is equivalent to not giving him enough face to grant him a yes. Since no one wants to slight anyone unnecessarily, those who put others into a position to say "no" are regarded as inconsiderate.

Thus before a person makes a request, he will generally send out a feeler in the form of a probe or hint. This can be done in many ways. For example, if a neighbour wants to borrow your lawnmower but is not sure how you would feel about the request, he may say something like this:

> "What a beautiful lawn you have! [flattery] I wish mine could be luscious like yours. Look at mine, it's overgrown and full of weeds. [humility: in reality it may just be slightly overgrown with a couple of dandelions] But what can I do? I wanted to buy a lawnmower but my garage is still full of boxes ... [hint]"

By this time, you would probably get the hint. If you do not mind lending your mower, you would offer yours without his asking. If you only want to help him out on a short term basis, you might suggest he build a garden shed, but mention that in the meantime he is free to use yours. If you do not want to lend out your machine, you can simply share his feelings about cluttered garages and leave it at that. In either case, neither you nor your neighbour will lose any face. You did not decline his request since no request was made.

Responding to a request, especially when a negative response is involved, can also be indirect. A common way to decline a request is to say "it is under consideration." In the North American culture, under consideration means exactly that. For many Chinese, however, it is just a polite way of saying "no". Some face is still lost but not as much as an outright "no". If a person truly wants to consider the matter, he would say something like "let me consider it and get back to you by tomorrow." In general, if a person defers a decision for an indefinite period of time, or needs to consult so-and-so but never raises the matter again, there is a very good chance that your request has been declined.

Although this indirect way of communication may come across as evasive or even insincere to Western ears, one must remember the intention is to save each other's face. To a person who is used to indirect communication, the message is perfectly clear and there is nothing insincere about protecting each other's face. To say the message directly without caring for the listener's feelings would be rude, something a person in a collectivist society tries to avoid at all costs. There is a Cantonese saying that captures the value of indirect communications: "When one is painting a portrait, there is no need to draw the person's intestines."

Besides face-saving, part of the evasiveness that Westerners perceive in the way many Chinese communicate may also be due to the linguistic structure of the Chinese language. Chinese permits plenty of ambivalence. Virtually every Chinese word when used on its own has multiple meanings. For example, the word *ji* ( 機 ) in Chinese can mean crisis, opportunities, chance, machines and airplanes, among other things. Sometimes the speaker will specify the exact meaning of a word by associating it with another word. In the above example, if the speaker says *jī huì* instead of just *jī*, he will surely mean "opportunity" and nothing else. Yet a speaker does not always clarify what he says, sometimes even intentionally. The recipient of a message will have to decide which meaning applies from the context.

Not every Chinese person uses indirect messages. Many are aware of the difference in this aspect between the East and the West. When speaking to North Americans, a lot of Chinese people will use direct messages. Still, if you have much contact with Chinese customers, you ought to keep your mind open to both as you will never know which style of communication your next customer is going to use. A good way to interpret your customer's message is to empty your mind and examine the situation. Then ask yourself: "Does what my customer tell me make sense in the context of this particular situation?"

## *The Three Photos in Alfred Chu's House*

Alfred Chu likes to decorate the walls of his house with framed photos of his family. He said this was the way his parents decorated their flat in Hong Kong. Some of the photos were taken more than a century ago and passed to him by his grandparents. Some are memories of Alfred's more recent past. Alfred has a story behind every one of those pictures. Walking through his house and listening to those stories is like walking through time.

Here are three of the photos in Alfred's collection:

### Photo A: Alfred and his teammates

Alfred is a cook in a Chinese restaurant. The picture shows all eight members of his cooking team, including the chef. The picture was taken in the sixties when they were still in training. Since then, they have continued working as a team. Together, they have served at some of the finest Chinese restaurants both in Hong Kong and Canada.

A good cooking team is the pillar of a Chinese restaurant. Unlike a Western restaurant, the chef, the cooks and the helpers are not hired individually. Instead, the cooking staff as a rule will join or leave the restaurant as a team. Each member of a team knows exactly how each other fits in in the kitchen, making it a very efficient work force.

The team's solidarity means more than efficiency. It also

means power and protection. They look out for each other's interests, negotiate salary and working conditions together, make decisions together, and sign contracts together. The concept is very much like the labour union, except a team is much smaller and more mobile. Even outside of work, the members of a team are generally very close to each other.

## Photo B: Alfred's family

This is one of the largest photos in Alfred's collection. The photo shows three rows of people all dressed in the style of the fifties. There were about forty people, and Alfred said this is his family photo.

In the middle of the front row sat an old man in a three-piece suit — Alfred's great grandfather, Mr. Chu Kai-jo. The picture was taken in Hong Kong on his eightieth birthday. Beside him were the old man's offspring and their spouses, most of them in their fifties and sixties. Alfred said the old man had eleven children altogether, but six of them had passed away by the time the picture was taken, and one had immigrated to Montreal. The third couple on the old man's right were Alfred's grandparents.

Standing in the second row were Alfred's parents, uncles and aunts. Alfred has so many uncles and aunts that some of them had to stand behind on the third row with the younger (Alfred's) generation. Some of his uncles and aunts were so young they were only children in the picture. Alfred names each one of them by their particular position in the family. This is no easy task as Chinese assign a particular term to each relative according to their specific relations and seniority. Thus addressing the father's third elder brother is different from addressing his second elder brother, which is also different from addressing his third younger brother.

On the third and last row were Alfred's peers and some of his younger uncles and aunts. Most of them were teenagers when the photo was taken. Some were so small they had to be held up by the older ones to show their faces. A couple of long time servants were also included. Alfred was about ten at the time, and was standing on the far left holding the hand of his nanny.

The family did not stay together under the same roof but lived in close proximity. At the time, the great grandfather was staying with his second eldest son (the eldest died during the Second World War). The old man died a few years after his eightieth birthday. Since then, other members of the older generations have also passed away, and many in the younger generations have immigrated to Canada. Alfred still visits them from time to time.

Alfred was expecting one of his nieces to join him next month. She would be coming to Canada as a foreign student, and would be staying at Alfred's house. Alfred was busy preparing the guest room for her stay. For Alfred, as well as for many Chinese, a niece is almost like a daughter.

## Photo C: The old man and the warlord

Alfred has an interesting story to tell about this picture. This is a picture of his great grandfather and one of the powerful warlords who ruled two southern Chinese provinces in the early part of the century. The picture was taken in the old man's home in Guǎngzhōu (Canton). Behind the two figures was a framed Chinese calligraph of a famous saying from Lǎo Zi (Lǎo Tzu): "If *Dào* (the Way) can be expressed in words, it is not the eternal *Dào*."

Alfred's great grandfather was a famous fortune-teller around the turn of the century. It was believed that he could foretell the outcome of a battle or commercial transaction weeks before it took place. Many military leaders and merchants came to him for advice, paying a high fee. One of those who sought advice from him was the warlord in the picture.

For a number of years, this warlord had been secretly planning to revolt against the weak central government. One of the things he did was to build up his airforce. It was said that at the time, he had the best airforce in the country. Finally an opportunity arose. The government forces were away. The warlord was ready to strike. Before he made his move, he consulted Alfred's great grandfather.

"What winds have brought your honourable body into my humble dwelling?" asked Chu Kai-jo. (Note the flattery and the self-deprecating style of speech.)

"I would not dare to step into your three-treasured palace if I didn't have something important to seek your advice!" replied the warlord.

"Please, please," said Chu.

"The government forces are away in the north. I'm worried their absence may make some people restless. Nowadays, there are bandits everywhere. Mr. Chu, please advise what I should do to calm the minds of the population?" (Note the lack of direct request for advice regarding a revolt.)

The message could not be clearer. Chu was put into a

dilemma. If he advised the warlord against a revolt, he might lose his life. If he advised him to revolt but the warlord lost in the end, he might also lose his life. Keeping his calm, Mr. Chu wrote these four characters on a piece of paper: *jī bù kě shī*. Translation: Don't miss the opportunity (*jī*).

The warlord was much encouraged by Chu's advice. He took the advisory note, and thanked Chu profusely before he left. The next day, he declared independence of the two provinces.

Within a week, his pilots revolted against him and flew the planes away. His revolt was pacified within a very short time. Just before his capture, the warlord re-read Mr. Chu's advisory note again to find out if he had misread anything. Nothing had been changed about the note. Yet this time he read another message from the same four characters: Don't lose (miss) the airplanes (*jī*).

[1] Lee, Kuan-yew. "Culture is Destiny," *Foreign Affairs*, March/April, 1994.

A glass sculpture of Buddha.
(Photo courtesy of Taipei Economic & Cultural Office)

# Chapter Five

# Chinese Beliefs, Taboos and Preferences

Many civilizations are founded on religious beliefs. The Western civilization is basically built on Christian principles and beliefs. The Islamic civilization is built on the teachings of the Koran. The Jewish culture centres around Judaism. The Chinese civilization, on the other hand, is built on a system of social ethics advocated by Confucius, instead of on a religious belief.

The Chinese people never have had a dominant religion. Throughout history, both Daoism and Buddhism had significant influence on the Chinese culture, but neither one had a greater influence over the other, and neither was able to replace Confucian thoughts. By the Sòng Dynasty, these three schools of thought were combined into a single philosophy known as neo-Confucianism. The synthesis of the three schools was a natural outcome for the Chinese, who have always taken a holistic approach to life.

Today, many Chinese people believe in elements of Confucianism, Daoism and Buddhism. For example, they may follow Confucius' code of ethics in social interactions, incorporate elements of Daoism, such as the concept of *yīn* and *yáng*, into anything from cooking to decorating the house, and then go to a Buddhist temple to pray or seek advice. Many can simultaneously practise Confucianism, Daoism, Buddhism and a number of folk religions without belonging to any of them. In fact, most Chinese people do not belong to any organized religion.

There is no rule about Chinese beliefs. Your next Chinese customer may describe himself as a Buddhist, but he also believes in *yīn yáng* and practises Confucius' code of ethics. He may belong to no religion but venerate his ancestors. He may also be a devoted Christian living with parents who practise idol worship and other folk religions. Many Chinese immigrants are Christians by conversion. The percentage of Christians among North American Chinese has been estimated to be as high as 20%. Your best policy is not to make any assumption about your customers but learn enough about each philosophy and religious belief to both respect and react to your customer's philosophy of life.

This chapter will examine Confucianism, Daoism, Buddhism and the folk religion practised by many Chinese. It will also describe some cultural preferences and taboos that may or may not be rooted in religious beliefs. Understanding your customers' belief system will make it easier for you to sense their likes and dislikes and respond to their wishes.

## *Confucianism*

It is impossible to speak of Chinese culture without making reference to Confucianism. It is, quite simply, the way Chinese people expect to relate and behave towards each other.

Confucianism is not a religion. It has no God, gods or forms of worship. It does not talk about heaven, hell or life after death. Rather it is a code of behaviour for leading an orderly social life.

Founded by Confucius in about 500 B.C., Confucianism has been expanded by many of his followers throughout the centuries, the most notable of them being Mencius, who lived in the fourth century B.C.

At the centre of Confucianism is the proper behaviour for a "gentleman." A gentleman is not just someone who is gentle, but one who has good moral character. A gentleman is loyal to his ruler, respectful of his parents and sincere to his fellows. A gentleman is expected to think for himself, study constantly and frequently conduct self-examination. A gentleman's behaviour is regulated by etiquette (*lǐ*) and guarded by a sense of righteousness (*yì*). He is not motivated by material rewards or threats of punishment, but by a sense of honour (*lián*) and shame (*chǐ*). In Confucius' terms: "A gentleman does not take advantage of the dark room."

Confucius believed if a gentleman is made a ruler, he can inspire his subjects to lead a moral life. He also believed that if a country is governed only by laws, the people will break the law whenever the opportunity presents itself. If a country is led by virtues, people will conduct themselves by their sense of honour without the threat of punishment. Since 200 B.C., his ideas have been adopted by many emperors as the essential subject of study before one could aspire to become a Mandarin, or government official, a much respected position in ancient China.

Thus Confucianism provides a moral framework for both personal and leadership ethics, and advocates that the two are intertwined. Following this view, the Chinese people believe those in leadership positions, from government to community to schools, must lead by moral authority. People not only have a duty to follow a leader's directions, but an even greater duty to renounce a leader when he is proven to be immoral. As Confucian scholar Professor Tu Wei-ming of Harvard University explained: "Confucianism is not simply the advocacy of obedience to government, but also the accountability of government."[1]

Confucius and his followers' ideas have been compiled into a large volume called *The Analects*, which effectively became the Bible of the Chinese way of moral behaviour. Confucius' concepts of respect for human dignity, fairness, etiquette and duty are still the underlying belief of many Chinese today, especially in business circles. The Golden Rule among the Chinese people goes like this: "What you don't wish for yourself, do not do to others." You will note its similarity to the Golden Rule of the Bible, though it is phrased less proactively.

### Daoism (also spelt as Taoism)

Daoism is both a philosophy and a religion. The philosophy first arose around 300 B.C., partly in reaction against Confucianism. Later it acquired elements of a number of Chinese folk religions and developed into a religion.

The philosophy of Daoism is recorded in the book *Dào Dé Jing* (also spelt *Tao Te Ching*) and the book of *Zhuāng Zi(Chuang Tzu)*. In contrast to Confucius' idea of orderly living with duties and rituals, Daoism advocates a spontaneous life free from social obligations. Its goal is to be in harmony with nature through simple living and meditation. The word *Dào*, or "The Way," means the way things are, or the reality as a whole, which constitutes all the individual ways. Daoists believe that "a truly good person is not aware of his goodness," and that "a truly effective person does nothing, but nothing will be left undone."

Daoists believe the Universe is composed of and is held together by two equal, opposite but complementary forces, the *yin* and the *yáng*. *Yin* is associated with darkness, the moon, femininity, tenderness, etc. *Yáng* is associated with brightness, the sun, masculinity, strength, etc. These two forces must be in harmony before anything can go right. This concept of duality has penetrated virtually every aspect of the Chinese living, from maintaining a healthful diet to running a business, whether or not the person believes in Daoism. For example, many Chinese, Daoist or not, believe the general health of a person depends on the balance between *yin* and *yáng* in his body. When one is not feeling well, it can always be attributed to the lack or excess of one of these two forces. The popular Chinese exercise, *Tai Chi*, is also based on the principle of duality.

Daoism was later influenced by Chinese folk religion and developed into a religion with divinities and priesthood. Some Daoists believe it is possible to attain immortality through meditation, special diet, breathing exercises and magic. Whether as a philosophy or as a religion, the Daoist principles have greatly influenced the Chinese literature, art, medicine and everyday life.

*Tai chi* is a popular exercise based on the *Daoist* principles of *yīn* and *yáng* (Photo courtesy of S.U.C.C.E.S.S.)

## Buddhism

Buddhism was introduced to China from India around A.D. 150 and became very popular a few hundred years later. Buddhism was founded by a Nepalese prince called Siddhartha Gautama. The term *Buddha*, meaning the Enlightened One, was a title given to him by his followers. When Guatama was 29, he had a series of visions which compelled him to leave his palace and family to seek enlightenment. At first he tried self-punishing exercises, and concluded that such practices could never lead to enlightenment. Then one day he gained enlightenment while meditating under a bodhi tree. Later, he began teaching his experience to others who became his followers.

The teaching of Buddha is called *dharma*. Central to Buddha's teaching is the cycle of death and rebirth. A person's well-being is determined by his or her behaviour in previous lives. Good behaviour will lead to a superior life or becoming a heavenly being in the next cycle, while poor behaviour will lead to an inferior life or even ending up in hell. For as long as a person is inside this cycle of death and rebirth, he or she will never be completely free of suffering. The way to break out of the cycle is to reach a state of complete happiness and peace called *Nirvana*. To reach this state, people must detach themselves from all desires and worldly possessions.

Whether one is a Buddhist or not, some of the Buddhist concepts have a great deal of influence on the Chinese way of thinking. For example, many Chinese believe what one sows today (*yīn*, or cause) determines what he or she will reap (*guǒ*, or effects) either in this lifetime or in lives to come. Another common belief is in the concept of *yuán (karma)*. This is a concept with no direct English equivalent. *Yuán* is a predetermined affinity between two people, the origin of which may be rooted in previous lives. When two people have *yuán* with each other, it is believed that chance will bring them together to become good friends or lovers.

## *Folk religion and ancestor veneration*

Chinese folk religion encompasses a broad range of veneration practices and idol worship. It is not an organized religion with priests and followers, but it is practised by many Chinese people in a variety of forms. Often elements of folk religion are incorporated into Daoism so that a Daoist priest may convey prayers to supernatural beings in the folk religion. Some Chinese may even treat folk religion, Daoism and Buddhism as a single religion.

The veneration practice generally involves paying homage to one or more supernatural beings. They may be legendary characters from folklore, heroes out of history, or personages believed to be able to protect them from evil and catastrophes. The common way to pay homage is to burn incense and offer food and rice wine in front of an icon or statue of the supernatural being. Often a Chinese family will have a special table or platform for these venerated icons. The location of this table or platform in relation to the main entrance and other furniture is thought to be important.

There are many venerated gods, spirits and supernatural guardians in Chinese folk religion. Here are a few of the most commonly venerated:

*Guān Dì:* He was a famous general in The Three Kingdoms (A.D. 221-263). He was not only a well-known warrior, but was much recognized for his loyalty. *Guān Dì* is venerated by many Chinese, notably business people and the police.

*Tŭ Dì Gōng:* The guardian of the land. It is believed that venerating him will bring peace and harmony to the land on which the household resides.

*Mén Shén:* The guardian of the door. Some traditional families will paste an icon of *Mén Shén* on their front doors to keep undesirable spirits from entering into the house.

An important group of supernatural guardians in many Chinese households are the ancestors. A family's ancestors are perhaps the most important of all venerated figures. The practice is partly based on the belief that ancestors will protect the household from evil and partly due to the deep respect Chinese people have for their ancestors. Even for those who do not practise veneration and do not believe in their ancestors' supernatural power, they still hold great respect for them. Nothing is more insulting to a Chinese than to insult his or her ancestors. At the same time, if a person is successful, he or she is said to have "brightened up the ancestors."

# Fēng shuǐ

There is a great deal of unnecessary mystery and misunder-standing about *fēng shuǐ*. To put it simply, *fēng shuǐ* is a holistic approach to site selection, landscaping, architecture and interior design to ensure the household will be in harmony with its surroundings. According to the principles of *fēng shuǐ*, the setting of a dwelling in relation to its environment can greatly influence the well-being of the household members, physically, mentally and financially. Some of the *fēng shuǐ* principles are based on common sense and experience, some are based on Daoist principles and folk religion, others are based on traditional preferences.

*Fēng shuǐ* in Chinese means "the wind and the water." Both the wind and water are components of the environment and both of them flow, reflective of the nature of *fēng shuǐ*. At the heart of *fēng shuǐ* are two invisible currents that flow through a dwelling: the *Qì* (also spelt *Ch'i*, pronounced as "chee") and the *Shà*. *Qì* is a beneficial current that is believed to flow along irregular paths. *Shà* is a malign current that is believed to flow in straight lines. The essence of *fēng shuǐ* is to maximize the flow and effects of *Qì* and minimize the flow and effects of *Shà* upon the household. To do so, *fēng shuǐ* masters have derived sets of rules to determine if the setting of a dwelling is beneficial to its occupants. Some of these rules are absolutes, others are relative to a number of factors, including the occupant's time of birth, direction of the main entrance and the geometric shape of the dwelling.

*Fēng shuǐ* masters use a special geomantic compass called *luó pán* to find the directions of a site and the key components of its surroundings, such as the contour and landmarks. It is believed that the contours and landmarks around a site will determine how the two invisible currents flow. For example, a site protected by mountains in the north and facing an open space in the south is generally considered beneficial, whereas a site facing the sharp edge of a pointed object, or the end of a blind alley, is generally considered malign. Within a dwelling, *fēng shuǐ* masters look at things such as the floor plan, the kitchen, the furniture arrangement, and even the placement of small decorating objects like statuettes and vases. Then they apply a set of rules to determine what is needed to be done in order to facilitate the flowing of *Qì*, and to counteract the effects of *Shà*.

Some of the rules used by *fēng shuǐ* masters have to do with the traditional Chinese belief in "the Principle of Five Elements." According to this principle, every substance, every colour and shape, every date and hour, every direction, every business, etc. can be categorized into one of these five elements: metal, wood, water, fire, earth (see Table 5.1). Each element is capable of

## Table 5.1
### The Five Elements of *Fēng Shuǐ*

| Element | Shape | Colour | Direction |
|---------|-------|--------|-----------|
| **Wood** | • Cylindrical<br>• Long, narrow | • Blue-green | • E<br>• SE |
| **Fire** | • Pointed | • Red | • S<br>• SW |
| **Earth** | • Flat<br>• Square | • Yellow | • NE |
| **Metal** | • Rounded | • White | • W<br>• NW |
| **Water** | • Irregular | • Black | • N |

generating another element according to the order specified in the Generative Cycle. It is also capable of destroying yet another element according to the order specified in the Destructive Cycle (see Figure 5.1). For example, Wood generates Fire and destroys Earth, Water generates Wood and destroys Fire, etc. Thus a tall and narrow building (considered to be Wood by shape) built on an irregular plot (considered to be Water by shape) is considered to

## Figure 5.1: Generative Cycle and Destructive Cycle

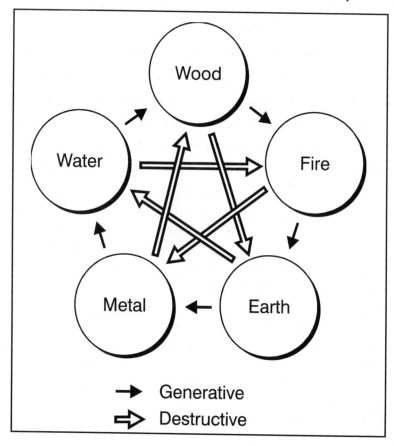

be beneficial since Water generates Wood. A pointed building (considered to be Fire by shape) built on the same plot is considered to be less than optimal since water destroys fire.

The *fēng shuǐ* rules can be very complicated. In addition, different *fēng shuǐ* masters may interpret the rules differently, leading to different recommendations.

## Yì tóu and the implication of numbers

Many Westerners are intrigued by the attention some Chinese people pay to certain numbers. This is especially so when it comes to getting a "good number" for one's house address, telephone number, bank account number and so on. It is a fairly well-recognized phenomenon that many Chinese customers prefer numbers with numerals 2, 3, and 8, and avoid the numeral 4.

These preferences are due to the concept of *yì tóu*. Again, here is a term that does not have a direct English equivalent. A way to understand *yì tóu* is to see it as a kind of premonition. Those who take *yì tóu* seriously believe that chance events or inadvertent remarks may be indicators of things to come. In this respect, it is similar to certain Western superstitions such as associating bad luck with seeing a black cat or with Friday the 13th. Thus a good wish from an innocent child or getting a good number by chance both have very good *yì tóu*, and are believed to bring in good luck. The reverse, such as getting a bad number, will have bad *yì tóu*, and are believed to cause bad luck. *Yì tóu* is not limited to numbers but applies to everything a person sees, hears or feels. More about *yì tóu* will be described in the following section on Taboos and Preferences. This section will concentrate on the application of *yì tóu* on numbers.

Why are 2, 3 and 8 regarded as good numerals and 4 as bad? The answer has a lot to do with how these numerals sound when pronounced in Chinese, especially Cantonese. Each numeral has a number of homonyms and the implications of some of these homonyms are not very desirable. The following table shows the pronunciations and homonyms for each numeral. The asterisks indicate that the homophony of Cantonese pronunciation is also recognized by Mandarin speakers.

### Table 5.2
### Chinese Numerals and Their Homonyms

| Numeral | Pronunciation in | | Homonyms |
|---------|------------------|----------|----------|
|         | *Cantonese*      | *Mandarin* |        |
| 1 | *Yud* | *Yī*\* | One, entirely\* |
| 2 | *Yee* | *Eì* | Easy |
| 3 | *Sarm* | *Sān* | Lively |
| 4 | *Say* | *Sì*\* | Dead, die\* |
| 5 | *Mm* | *Wǔ*\* | Not, negative\* |
| 6 | *Look* | *Liù* | Road, way |
| 7 | *Chut* | *Qī* | Definite, surely |
| 8 | *Bard* | *Bā* | Prosperous |
| 9 | *Gow* | *Jiǔ*\* | Long lasting\* |
| 0 | *Ling* | *Líng* | No special homonym |

With the understanding of these homonyms and the concept of *yì tóu*, you will now see why many Chinese people prefer 2 (easy), 3 (lively) and 8 (prosperous), and avoid 4 (death). Even those who do not believe in *yì tóu* may not like to have a number that sounds like death and dying. If your numbering system had the same homonyms, even if you were not superstitious, how

### Table 5.3
### Combinations with Desirable Implications

| Number | Implied Meaning |
|--------|-----------------|
| 12 | Certainly easy |
| 13 | Certainly lively |
| 23 | Easy to be lively |
| 28 | Easy to prosper |
| 32 | Business |
| 33 | Very lively |
| 78 | Surely to be prosperous |
| 79 | Surely to last long |
| 82 | Prosperous and lively |
| 88 | Prosperous for a long time |
| 128 | Will surely get rich |
| 138 | Be prosperous the entire life |
| 168 | Be prosperous all the way |
| 222 | Easy, easy, easy |
| 333 | Lively, lively, lively |
| 888 | Prosperous, prosperous, prosperous |

## Table 5.4

### Combinations with Undesirable Implications

| Number | Implied Meaning |
|--------|-----------------|
| 14 | Surely die |
| 24 | Easy to die |
| 44 | Die, die |
| 46 | Way to die, also slang for male sexual organ |
| 47 | Surely to die |
| 51 | Will not move |
| 53 | Not lively |
| 58 | Will not prosper |
| 59 | Will not last long |
| 67 | Derogatory reference to male sexual organ |
| 69 | Derogatory reference to male sexual organ |
| 74 | Surely die |
| 164 | All the way to death |
| 5354 | Silly meaningless things |

would you like to live in a house numbered "surely die surely die?"

Combinations of numerals also have special meanings due to homonyms. Tables 5.3 and 5.4 list the numerical combinations some people prefer and others they avoid.

It is important to know that not all Chinese people pay attention to numbers. Many of them will have no objection to getting an undesirable number. At the same time, not every customer will tell you he or she prefers to have a good number. Some may feel it improper or feel embarrassed to ask for one. One strategy you may try is to offer them a choice of a few numbers, with at least one or two "good combinations."

## Taboos and preferences

Every culture has its taboos and preferences, and the Chinese culture is no exception. Most taboos in Chinese culture are directly or indirectly related to death and sex. If you stay away from these two topics, you can generally avoid getting yourself into unpleasant situations. At the same time, Westerners do not need to be overly concerned about inadvertently offending Chinese friends as most of them understand that you do not know. An offence made out of ignorance will generally be forgiven.

This section describes some of the more traditional taboos and preferences. It must be emphasized that not all Chinese people share the same beliefs. Moreover, as time changes, what was once a taboo can quickly become an acceptable practice. This is especially so for many North American Chinese since they are adjusting to the Western culture everyday.

### Colours

Many people know the Chinese regard bright red as a colour that will bring in good fortune. Red is especially desirable when used as a base colour for invitation cards and sometimes promotional materials. Often information on these cards is printed in gold, both for contrast and for its implied wealth. Bright red and gold are used a lot in traditional ceremonies. Suppliers, however, should not overuse these colours as they may lose their effect and come across as patronizing to some Chinese. To understand why this may be so, imagine you are reading a book in which every word is printed in bold, capitalized and double-underlined.

White is generally regarded as a colour of mourning. Nevertheless, most Chinese are used to the idea of writing on white paper, wearing white shirts and living in a house with white walls. Unless white is used in a ceremonial setting or in a special type of clothing, it is generally regarded as a neutral background colour instead of a taboo.

There are two colours you may want to avoid: pale yellow and pale blue. These two colours are used a lot in traditional Chinese funerals and are often referred to as "dead person's yellow" and the "dead person's blue." You probably will not get an overly enthusiastic response from your Chinese customers if your promotional materials are printed on paper in these colours.

## Clothing

Although Chinese have their traditional clothing, they usually wear it only at ceremonies or banquets. Generally these are garments made of silk or a special silky material called *Duàn* with a good deal of embroidery. Such garments are rarely worn in everyday life.

Stay away from long white robes and white or black headbands. These are mourning garments.

Do not give out or ask your customers to put on a green hat. "A man wearing a green hat" in the Chinese culture implies his wife is sleeping with someone else. On the other hand, Westerners have no need to refrain from wearing green hats if they wish.

Your Chinese customers may quietly giggle, but what you put on your own head does not insult them or their spouses.

## Conversation topics

Sex is a forbidden topic in social conversations. This includes off-coloured jokes, someone's private life, or description of a sexually explicit show. This is not to say that Chinese people do not enjoy this aspect of life, but most of them are uncomfortable talking about it openly. This is especially so between people of opposite genders, even if the information conveyed is clearly a joke.

Refrain from commenting on the attractiveness of your customer's appearance, especially customers of the opposite sex. Comments like this can be misconstrued in a culture that frequently uses indirect communications. Similarly, do not comment on the look of the customer's spouse, even if you want to send him or her a compliment.

## Other taboos

Some other taboos, mostly relating to table manners and gift giving, will be discussed in Chapter 13.

## A Sunday Afternoon with Lau's Family

K.K. Lau is a new immigrant to Canada. A few years ago his son Kelly came to Canada to study. Shortly after Kelly finished his studies, K.K. Lau and the rest of his family came to join him in British Columbia. They bought a house in Richmond.

I call K.K. by the name of "Uncle Lau." K.K is not really my uncle, but a good friend of my father. For the Chinese, it is customary to refer to family friends of one's parents as "uncles" and "aunts." The terms are more than a matter of formality. They do convey a sense of respect according to Confucius' principles of respecting the elders.

One Sunday afternoon, I decided to pay Uncle Lau a visit. We agreed to meet at the Richmond Chinese Buddhist Temple where he and his family were to have lunch. Every Sunday Uncle Lau and his family come to the temple to pray and then stay for a vegetarian lunch.

The temple is open all week with no scheduled services. People simply come to pray or pay homage to the statues symbolizing Buddha and some of his early followers, and then leave whenever they wish. Uncle Lau chooses to come on Sundays because this is the day he can meet more people. Occasionally they offer seminars by reputed Buddhist monks and scholars.

When I arrived, the parking lot was full. There was a preponderance of numeral 8 on the licence plates of parked cars. It seems that numerals in Chinese-owned licence plates do not necessarily follow the law of random distribution. After passing a few vehicles bearing 888 in their plates, I reached the main building.

The temple adopts a Chinese architectural style with a dragon head carved at each corner of its roof. The air of the temple was filled with the smell of burning incense and the low hum of people reciting *sutras*, or Buddhist scriptures. Inside the main hall, a number of people were lighting incense sticks and paying homage to the statues in the middle of the hall. The statues were not particularly large, only a few times larger than life. Some Buddhist temples elsewhere in the world have statues hundreds of feet tall. At one corner I saw a nun in yellow robes sitting on the floor, reciting *sutras* repeatedly with a chain of beads hanging from her right palm.

I saw both Uncle and Auntie Lau raise a bunch of lighted incense sticks over their heads, bow to one of the statues, then insert the sticks into the holder. At this point Uncle Lau saw me and smiled. We went to the lunch hall together. Only vegetarian dishes are served in a Buddhist temple.

"Kelly and Mary (Lau's children) are at the church," Uncle Lau said, referring to a Chinese Christian church to which Kelly belongs. "Nowadays, the younger generations have their own ways. I have no objection to their belonging to the Christian faith. I think all religions are telling people to do good things. They even invited us to one of their meetings the other evening."

Over lunch, Uncle Lau brought me the latest news about my father in Hong Kong, about his health, the birds he keeps, and the morning *Tai Chi* exercises they did together.

"He also asked me to bring you two pieces of jade," Uncle Lau said, "but I left them at home. Do you mind coming to my home to pick them up after lunch?"

My father is a jade collector. He has jade pieces of all kinds. Chinese people like jade for its beauty and brilliance. It is also believed that jade can guard one from evil. Every time a friend visits Canada, my father will ask him to bring me some pieces of his collection. After lunch we went to Uncle Lau's house together. Along the way he pointed at a house located at the end of a T-junction.

"You know what? Kelly almost bought this house before we came!" Uncle Lau spoke with passion. Mildly shaking his head, he continued: "It's a good thing he listened to us, otherwise we would all be stuck in that place, and who knows what would have happened."

Then he went on telling me why the house has poor *fēng shuǐ*, and why it is not desirable to live in houses like that.

"I know Kelly doesn't believe in *fēng shuǐ*, and he said the house is at least twenty thousand dollars cheaper than market price. But what is twenty thousand dollars compared to peace of mind?"

"Well at least in the end he listened to you. You shouldn't be too harsh on your son," Auntie Lau interjected.

Within minutes we were at Uncle Lau's house. His house is located in a new sub-division in Richmond. There was a fair-sized lawn at the front with some small shrubs and a couple of junipers. In the middle of the lawn was a conspicuous circle of bare soil. Uncle Lau must have read the puzzled look on my face.

"There was a tree on that spot, but I had it moved to the backyard. The tree was nice but it was right in front of the door. Bad *fēng shuǐ*, you know. The gardener said he's going to put turf on that spot next week."

I waited in the living room while Uncle Lau went to get the jade pieces. The decoration of his living room is very typically Chinese. There was a large fine Chinese carpet in the middle, with rosewood furniture on two sides. Hanging on the wall were some Chinese paintings and a couple of calligraphy. One of the calligraphy featured the well-known "House Rules According to Zhū Xǐ" which started with this sentence:

"Wake up early in the morning to clean up the courtyard."

Zhū Xǐ was a reputed scholar in the *Sòng* Dynasty who synthesized the essence of various schools of thought, including Confucianism, Daoism and Buddhism, into an integrated philosophy, later known as neo-Confucianism.

At one corner of the living room there was a small table. On it were two rectangular wooden plaques. One plaque had the drawings of three human figures, with *Guān Dì*, the famous general in The Three Kingdoms, in the middle. The other plaque had the Chinese inscriptions: "All of The Lau's Ancestors." Uncle Lau has always been very proud of his ancestors and the name Lau. After all, the Lau family (In Mandarin the word is "Liú") ruled China during the *Hàn* Dynasty. Lau is therefore regarded as one of the emperor's surnames. In front of the plaque was an incense holder and a couple of plates of fruit and cakes. Under the tall table on the floor was another plaque and another incense holder.

The plaque said: "*Tŭ Dì* (Guardian of the Land) from all directions."

Uncle Lau came back with two pieces of jade of equal sizes. Each was a rectangular piece with a string attached through an axis drilled along its entire length. One piece was uniformly light green, almost whitish. The other piece was uniformly dark green. Both were translucent without a speck of imperfection. Even in indirect lighting they showed a great deal of brilliance. I learned enough about jade from my father to recognize their value.

"This is a pair of *yīn yáng* jade blocks from Burma. Your father asked you to wear them all the time. They will protect you from all evil," Uncle Lau said.

I smiled. I know I will wear them and protect them from all evil.

---

Chinese celebrations are often highlighted with dragon dancing.
Movie star Jackie Chan takes part in a dragon dance in
Vancouver, B.C.
(Photo courtesy of S.U.C.C.E.S.S.)

# Chapter Six

# *F*estivals and Celebrations

Chinese people celebrate a number of festivals at different times of the year. Three are especially important: Chinese New Year, Dragon Boat Festival and Mid-Autumn Festival. Besides being a time for celebration, these festivals are also time for the Chinese to build or strengthen relationships with friends and associates. Unlike most festivals in other cultures, none of the major Chinese festivals have religious origins.

For the business community, these festivals mean good opportunities, much like Christmas and Valentine's Day in the West. Many firms have conducted special promotions during these festivals with great results. Understanding the significance of these festivals can show that you are interested in your customers' culture. It can also help you identify good business opportunities.

## *Chinese New Year*

The Chinese New Year takes place on the first day of the first month of the Chinese lunar calendar, usually some time in February. The lunar calendar has 12 months of 29 or 30 days each. The days of a month are dictated by the lunar phase. Thus the first of each month has a thin crescent, while the fifteenth has a full moon. During the leap year, which occurs seven times in a

19-year period, a whole month is added to the year rather than a day. The lunar calendar has been used in China for centuries and was the basis for timing the various farming activities.

There are many folklore legends associated with the origin of the New Year. A popular one goes like this: Once upon a time, an awful animal called *Nián* (meaning "Year") would visit the peasants once a year, causing great disruptions and fear. The peasants would light firecrackers to scare the animal away. Once *Nián* retreated, the peasants would all come out to celebrate its departure and wish each other well for the rest of the year. Although the majority of the Chinese people do not take these legends seriously, the festival itself is still the most celebrated event of the year. In many parts of Asia, people celebrate Chinese New Year for seven days.

Days before the New Year, people clean their homes, shop for new clothes, get their hair cut and prepare special foods for the occasion. They also decorate their homes and offices. While decorations vary from setting to setting, most people put up some *chūn lián* on their walls or doors. A *chūn lián* is a well-wish written on a sheet of red paper. The well-wishes are usually related to the health, peace and prosperity of the family members. They also fill their houses or stores with live peach blossoms and *Kumquat* plants.

Actual celebration starts on the evening before New Year's Day. A custom many Chinese observe is to stay awake all night on New Year's Eve and to keep a light switched on all through the night. The practice is believed to bring health and long life to the parents. All members of a family have dinner together, much like the custom of having Christmas and Thanksgiving dinners. Typically on New Year's Eve, employers hand out bonuses or double pay to their workers.

On New Year's Day, no one cleans house or goes to work. Instead, people put on their new clothes and go out visiting. There are many ways to greet each other and the most common one is *"gung hay fat choy"* (Cantonese) or *"gōng xǐ fā cái"* (Mandarin). The literal translation of this greeting is "wishing you to be prosperous," although the message is "Happy New Year." This is a perfect example of Chinese sentences that carry completely different messages than their literal meaning.

The day after New Year's Day is traditionally known as *kāi nián*, meaning The Beginning of the Year. This is the day when business officially starts again. To celebrate, wherever the law allows,[1] store owners light firecrackers in front of their stores. There will be lion dancing in the streets of most communities. Celebrations go on for a few more days. During this time, people visit their friends and relatives. They give each other's unmarried children *hóng bāo*, a small sum of money in a red packet (Cantonese people call it *ligh see*, or "lucky money.") There is no rule as to how much one should give. Often the amount depends on the relationship between the giver and the recipient. They serve the visitors special dried fruits, dried lotus and watermelon seeds. The seventh day into the New Year is called *rén rì*, meaning the Day of People, or Everyone's Birthday. On this day, for ceremonial purposes, everyone will be a year older.[2]

The Chinese New Year provides plenty of opportunities for North American business people who want to address the local

A dragon boat racing in mid-stream. Dragon boat racing is now an annual event in many parts of the world.
(Photo courtesy of Taipei Economic & Cultural Office)

Chinese market. Here are some suggestions for your consideration:

- Enhance your corporate image by sponsoring and participating in Chinese New Year events.
- If your business is run exclusively by Chinese employees, you may consider giving them a year-end bonus on Chinese New Year's Eve.
- Decorate your storefront or office for the occasion.
- Offer New Year's greetings in Chinese.
- Provide dried fruits, lotus and watermelon seeds.
- Have a special promotion on Chinese New Year, such as using lion dance to attract customers to your storefront.
- Hand out coupons in a red packet.
- Visit your customers and associates to strengthen your relationship.

To what extent you adopt them will depend on the nature of your business, your employee and customer compositions, and budgetary constraints.

## *Dragon Boat Festival*

This Festival takes place on the fifth day of the fifth month according to the Chinese lunar calendar, usually some time in June.

The Dragon Boat Festival commemorates a minister-poet called Qū Yuán, a respected counsellor to the king of one of the states in China during the Warring Period (403-227 B.C.) Qū Yuán eventually fell out of favour and committed suicide by drowning himself in the river. On hearing the news of his death, peasants raced out to the middle of the river in an attempt to retrieve his

Celebration of the birthday of the Heavenly Queen, *Tin Hau*, in Hong Kong.
Though a lesser event compared to the Chinese New Year, it is much
celebrated along the coastal areas of China, especially by fishermen.
(Photo courtesy of Kiu Chan)

body but without success. They also threw food into the river, hoping that well-fed fish would not devour Qū Yuán's body.

Ever since then, Chinese people have raced their boats in rivers, lakes and oceans every year on this date. The boats later evolved into the famous dragon boats, which are long canoe-shaped boats with a dragon head carved at the front. For the occasion, people also prepare a special type of food called *zòng zi*. This is a serving of rice and other ingredients such as meat or beans wrapped and cooked in a special leaf. The leaf both adds flavour to and preserves the freshness of the food.

Dragon boat racing is now a highly visible international event. Many companies, Chinese or otherwise, take part in it. It is an excellent occasion to publicize your company's image, either by taking part in the race, or by helping to sponsor the event.

## Mid-Autumn Festival

This festival takes place on the fifteenth day of the eighth month in the Chinese calendar, generally around the beginning of September. The festival is sometimes referred to as the Moon Festival because in the lunar calendar, the fifteenth day of a month always has a full moon, and the eighth month generally has clear skies.

The fifteenth day of the eighth month was the date the Chinese people revolted against the Mongols at the end of the Yuán dynasty (A.D. 1279-1368). Before the uprising, the Chinese people coordinated their moves by hiding messages inside cakes they sent to one another as gifts. The resulting revolution was a stunning success. The Chinese regained control of their homeland

A Chinese wedding in traditional costume.
(Photo courtesy of Taipei Economic & Cultural Office)

and started the Míng Dynasty (A.D. 1368-1644).

To this date, Chinese still celebrate the occasion. Days before the festival, they start giving each other mooncakes made of lotus seeds and egg yokes. On the day of the festival, people put out lanterns and gather together to "appreciate the moon." They eat mooncakes and other festive food items. For fun, youngsters roam the streets with lanterns in their hands.

There are many ways you can celebrate with your Chinese customers. You can offer pieces of mooncake and other food items around the time of the festival at your stores or offices. You can visit your Chinese business contacts to offer them a box of mooncakes as a way to strengthen your ties with them. You can organize a special sale targeted to the Chinese customers and call it the Moon Festival sale. You can decorate your stores or offices with lanterns to show your appreciation for the event. You can also organize a moon appreciation party for your staff, customers and families. The possibilities are unlimited.

## Other festivals

There are other festivals in the Chinese culture, but they do not have as much commercial value as the three listed above. Below is a brief summary of three minor festivals.

### Qing Míng Festival

This festival occurs usually around April. This is the day when the Chinese visit and clean up their ancestors' tombs.

## The Seventh Sister's Festival

On the evening of the seventh day of the seventh month, unmarried women gather together to make their wishes to a couple of legendary lovers. The practice is based on a romantic story in Chinese folklore which involves a pair of lovers who were forbidden by the Heavenly Queen to see each other except once a year. To keep them apart, she turned them into two stars on opposite sides of the Milky Way. (The Chinese call it "The Silvery River," or *yín hé*.) Once a year, the birds would make a bridge across the Silvery River so that the couple could meet.

## The Double Nine Festival

This takes place on the ninth day of the ninth month, generally in October. The festival originated from a legend of a family in ancient China. The family was forewarned by an old man that a calamity would befall their household on this day. The only way to escape was to climb up a high mountain. The family did as the old man suggested. When they returned, they found all their domestic animals had died of unknown causes. Since then, the Chinese climb up to high places on this day every year. Many make use of the opportunity to visit and clean up their ancestors' tombs before winter sets in.

## The Day When BC TEL Introduced
## Their Services in Chinese

To many Canadians, the day was an ordinary Saturday in September, 1994. To the Chinese, it was the Mid-Autumn Festival. To BC TEL, it was the day service in the Chinese language was first introduced to their customers.

Providing service in Chinese was a logical response to the changing demographics of BC TEL's customer base. Since the beginning of the nineties, the Chinese population in British Columbia has been growing by an average of 10% to 12% a year, making it the second largest ethnic group in the Greater Vancouver Regional District, next to the British. The move involved providing services in Chinese at two of its retail outlets, the telesales and customer services divisions.

For a company that has always provided services in only one language, the move is significant both for BC TEL and for its customers. The company decided to kickoff the event from its retail outlet at Richmond, B.C., where one in three residents is Chinese, on the day of the Mid-Autumn Festival. Days before, the event had been well-advertised in the Chinese media.

The retail outlet, called BC TEL Communication Centre, is located in the Richmond Centre, one of the busiest shopping centres in the province. On this Saturday the communication centre was decorated with lanterns. Chinese signs were erected,

137

sending a strong signal to the Chinese community that BC TEL now speaks their language. Inside the store, some smiling new faces, all Asians, were working side by side with Caucasians.

Around noon time, a Chinese radio station came to cover the event. At first the newscaster set up the microphone at the mall's entrance, and later decided to move to the front of store. Onlookers began to accumulate, and some entered the store to shop for bargains. Then in a dramatic move, amidst the sound of drumbeats, a troupe of lion dancers emerged to start the kickoff. The crowd cheered. The event was a smashing success. In one afternoon, between four and five thousand shoppers almost cleared out the entire inventory, even though the store was not holding a sale. Never before has any BC TEL retail outlet been sold out of inventory. The day made history. Since then, for a number of months, the Richmond Communication Centre has been the top performer among BC TEL's 37 retail outlets.

No one could be more pleased than Thomas Leung, Director, International Market at BC TEL. He predicts that BC TEL's involvement in the ethnic communities will grow.

"BC TEL's mission is to make it easy for people to exchange information anywhere, anytime. Providing services in the Chinese language will make it easy for the 260,000 Chinese people in B.C. to exchange information," he said.

What is more, the company plans to extend similar services to other ethnic groups.

"It is BC TEL's intent to provide services to other ethnic groups in their languages, whenever the numbers warrant. At this point we're already working on providing a similar package to our Punjabi customers and two other ethnic groups," Leung added.

Asked why he timed the kickoff to coincide with the Mid-Autumn Festival, he explained: "The Mid-Autumn Festival is a time of celebration for the Chinese. Timing the event and the festival together confirms our commitment and respect for our Chinese customers. It sends the message that BC TEL wants to celebrate this occasion with them by introducing a much-needed service."

Leung said that it is always BC TEL's policy to put money into the community:"Getting involved in the Chinese community events, festivals and festivities is only one example. Every year, we participate in the Chinese New Year Fair. BC TEL has its own team which races at the Dragon Boat Festival. Other than taking part in Chinese festivals, we also support a number of fund-raising campaigns with high Chinese exposure, such as the Mount Saint Joseph Hospital, and the annual Walk with the Dragon sponsored by S.U.C.C.E.S.S."

---

[1] Firecrackers have been outlawed in Hong Kong since 1967.

[2] According to the traditional Chinese way of calculating age, everyone is already a year old on the date he or she is born. Then everyone gains another year on the Seventh Day of the New Year. Thus a person born on the Sixth Day of the Year will be two years old the next day. This type of calculation is rarely used in everyday life now for its obvious confusion, but is still used from time to time for ceremonial purposes.

# Part II

## $\mathscr{R}$eaching Your Customers

*"Winning is always preceded of much
calculations at the headquarters."*

— Sun Tzu, an ancient Chinese military strategist

# $\mathscr{I}$ntroduction to Part II

Marketing to your Chinese customers is fundamentally no different from marketing to any other customer group. You must start with the right products with the right values at the right price. You must have good planning, good marketing information and a good implementation strategy. All the rules that apply to targeted marketing also apply to marketing your products to the Chinese consumers. As editor-in-chief of Marketing Magazine Wayne Gooding puts it: "Ethnic marketing is just a kind of targeted marketing."

Part II of the book deals with reaching out to the Chinese customers. Like all other forms of marketing, reaching the Chinese customers requires information, analysis, planning and implementation. Chapter Seven provides some marketing information about the Chinese population in Canada, and resources for obtaining additional information. Chapter Eight discusses the general analysis and planning processes involved in reaching out to Chinese consumers. Chapter Nine describes some of the strategies that have been successfully employed by certain firms.

Newcomers receiving help with immigration document
— an important source of immigration statistics.
(Photo courtesy of Kiu Chan)

# Chapter Seven

# *M*arketing Information

## *A leap of faith*

In successful marketing, information is king. The more you know about your customers, the more effectively you can direct your resources to address their needs. On this point, however, suppliers will quickly get into a dilemma: unlike the mainstream market, information about the Chinese market segment is not as complete and not as readily available. Suppliers will either have to work with insufficient information and take a leap of faith in order to get the first move advantage, or to spend valuable time studying the situation to their satisfaction, and risk missing the window of opportunity.

This chapter provides answers to three basic questions about the Chinese market segment in Canada:

- What are the immigration, demographic and socio-economic facts we have about the Chinese market?
- What consumer information is available and where can we get it?
- How can we obtain additional information?

Since the overwhelming majority of the Chinese Canadian population resides in Toronto and Vancouver, this chapter will concentrate on these two metropolitan areas. Unless otherwise specified, the information in this chapter was provided by DJC Research of Toronto,** a subsidiary of Nielsen Marketing Research. Information in this chapter will help you assess whether you would like to take a leap of faith, or to conduct additional research before making a move.

## *Market size*

Until results of the 1996 Census are available, the size of the Chinese market can only be estimated. Using recognizable Chinese surnames in the telephone directories in Toronto and Van-

### Table 7.1
### Market Size Estimate

|  | *Total* | *Toronto* | *Vancouver* |
|---|---|---|---|
| Total households | 129,350 | 79,250 | 50,100 |
| Total individuals | 501,550 | 301,150 | 200,400 |
| Under 18 years old | 108,550 | 65,100 | 43,450 |
| 18-34 years old | 177,700 | 112,350 | 65,350 |
| 35 years and older | 215,300 | 123,700 | 91,600 |
| Total male adults | 193,400 | 117,400 | 76,000 |
| 18-34 years old | 86,900 | 55,150 | 31,750 |
| 35 years and older | 106,500 | 62,250 | 44,250 |
| Total female adults | 199,600 | 118,650 | 80,950 |
| 18-34 years old | 90,800 | 57,200 | 33,600 |
| 35 years and older | 108,800 | 61,450 | 47,350 |

*Source: DJC Research 1993-1995*

couver, DJC Research conducted a survey of Chinese households in 1994. The survey asked respondents to list the gender and age of each person in the household. Table 7.1 summarizes the results.

Other estimates, using information supplied by various municipalities, or from business databases, have placed the 1994 population of Chinese in Toronto to be between 300,000 and 350,000, and in Vancouver to be between 200,000 and 260,000.

## Geographic distribution

Not only do most of the Chinese Canadian live in and around Toronto and Vancouver, they also concentrate in a relatively small number of areas in these two cities. In Toronto, over 70% of the Chinese live in Scarborough, City of Toronto and North York. In Vancouver, over 75% of the Chinese live in the City of Vancouver, Richmond and Burnaby. Figure 7.1 shows the geographic distribution of the Chinese people in these two metropolitan areas.

Note that this distribution is changing all the time, due to the continual arrival of newer immigrants and relocation. As an example, the Chinese populations of Richmond, B.C. and Markham, Ontario have expanded significantly since the study was done. A reliable updated figure was not available at press time.

## Chinese immigration to Canada

Chinese began immigrating to Canada before the turn of the century. The first Chinese came to help build the Canadian Pacific Railroad. Subsequent immigration, until 1947, was greatly discouraged first by the head tax and later by the Chinese

## Figure 7.1: Geographic Distribution of Chinese People in Toronto and Vancouver

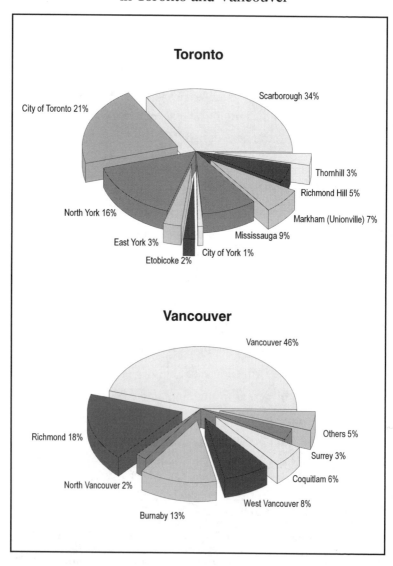

**Toronto**

Scarborough 34%

City of Toronto 21%

Thornhill 3%

Richmond Hill 5%

Markham (Unionville) 7%

North York 16%

Mississauga 9%

East York 3%

City of York 1%

Etobicoke 2%

**Vancouver**

Vancouver 46%

Others 5%

Richmond 18%

Surrey 3%

Coquitlam 6%

North Vancouver 2%

West Vancouver 8%

Burnaby 13%

Exclusion Act. Since these early immigrants and their descendants have already adjusted to Canadian society, it can be assumed that their consumer habits are no longer distinguishable from the rest of Canadians. This section will therefore concentrate on the immigration pattern after 1947, when the Chinese Exclusion Act was lifted.

Immigration after 1947 is more like a series of distinct waves than a steady stream. For example, in 1967, probably as a result of the Cultural Revolution in China, the Communists instigated a riot and civil disturbance in Hong Kong that lasted for months. Life eventually returned to normal but the incident caused a great deal of concern to many people, sparking a wave of emigration in the subsequent years. In 1989, the Chinese government suppressed a pro-democratic and anti-corruption movement headed by students and workers. Many people died during the incident, which sparked another wave of emigration both from China and Hong Kong. Each wave brought in immigrants from different socio-economic backgrounds with different skills. Table 7.2 summarizes the patterns of immigration to Canada since 1947. You will note that the Chinese people came to Canada at different times from different places for different reasons, which explains the vast diversity within the Chinese community in Canada.

Most recently, the Canadian federal government announced its 1996 immigration quota to be slightly less than 200,000. Certain immigration categories, such as business immigrants, will be encouraged. Many immigration observers expect the flow of immigrants from Hong Kong, Taiwan and China to continue unabated.

Figure 7.2 shows the number of new Chinese immigrants in

149

## Table 7.2
### Events in Asia and Chinese Immigration 1947-1995

| Period | Primary Event |
|---|---|
| 1947-67 | Family reunification |
| 1967 | Riot in Hong Kong |
| 1967-80 | Surge of students and professionals from Hong Kong |
| 1978 | Start of economic reform in China[1] |
| 1980-85 | Surge of immigrants from China following economic reform |
| 1985-89 | First wave of immigrants from Hong Kong due to 1997 deadline |
| 1989 | *Tiānānmén* Square massacre |
| 1989-95 | Continued inflow of immigrants from Hong Kong, China and Taiwan |

four of Canada's provinces between 1991 and 1995.

Besides population figures, three additional pieces of information will be very useful: their countries of last residency, how long they have been in Canada and the immigration category they fall under. Learning about where your customers are from and how long they have been in Canada can help you relate to them and make decisions, such as language and brand name selection. Learning about their immigration category can give an indication of their purchasing power, and their likelihood of setting up a business in Canada.

There are three main classes of immigrants — family class, refugees and business immigrants. According to Citizenship and

Immigration Canada, they are defined as follows:

*Family class* immigrants are sponsored spouses, fiancés, dependent children, parents and grandparents of Canadian citizens or permanent residents, who agreed to support them while they settle in Canada.

*Refugees* are people fleeing persecution and seeking Canada's protection. They can be sponsored by the government or by private citizens, or those who have claimed refugee status upon arrival and whose claims have been determined to be valid.

*Business immigrants* include self-employed persons, entrepreneurs and investors, along with their dependents. *Self-employed* persons intend to establish a business that will create an employment

### Fig. 7.2: Number of New Chinese Immigrants in Four of Canada's Provinces between 1991 and 1995

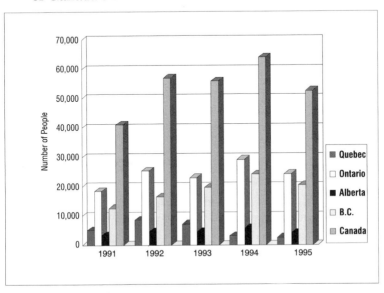

opportunity for themselves. *Entrepreneurs* intend to establish, purchase or invest in a business in Canada which will create at least one job for Canadians. *Investors* must make a minimum investment in a Canadian business which will contribute to employment opportunities for Canadians.

In a survey covering about 1,000 Chinese household decision-makers, DJC Research found that 95% of the Chinese in Toronto and 93% in Vancouver were born outside of Canada, indicating an overwhelming majority of the Chinese people in Canada are immigrants. Table 7.3 summarizes their country of last permanent residence, years in Canada, and classes of immigration.

### Socio-economic indicators

In another study involving over 1,500 Chinese Canadians in Toronto and Vancouver, DJC Research compared certain key characteristics of the Chinese population with those of the general population.[2] Here are the highlights of their results:

- Relatively more Chinese are under 45 years old (64%) than the general population (56%).
- There are more single Chinese (36%) than the general population (26%) in both cities.
- There are fewer divorced/widowed Chinese (3% in Toronto; 4% in Vancouver) than the general population (15% in Toronto; 18% in Vancouver).
- More Chinese household financial decision-makers have post-secondary education (59% in Toronto; 56% in Vancouver) than those of the general population (48% in Toronto; 52% in Vancouver).
- More Chinese household financial decision-makers own

# Table 7.3
## Immigration Background

| | Percentage | |
| --- | --- | --- |
| | *Toronto* | *Vancouver* |
| **Last Permanent Residence** | | |
| Hong Kong | 56 | 56 |
| China | 21 | 19 |
| Taiwan | 6 | 13 |
| Vietnam | 2 | 1 |
| U.S.A. | 3 | 2 |
| Malaysia | 2 | 1 |
| Others | 10 | 8 |
| **Years in Canada** | | |
| Less than 3 years | 21 | 23 |
| 3 to 4 years | 24 | 24 |
| 5 to 10 years | 32 | 28 |
| 11 to 15 years | 10 | 10 |
| 16 years or more | 13 | 15 |
| **Class of Immigration** | | |
| Family | 35 | 28 |
| Independent | 33 | 26 |
| Business | | |
|     Investor | 9 | 16 |
|     Entrepreneur | 4 | 10 |
|     Self-employed | 1 | 1 |
| Assisted Relative | 6 | 8 |
| Retired | 3 | 4 |
| Others | 9 | 7 |

*Source: DJC Research 1993-1995*

their homes (69% in Toronto; 82% in Vancouver) than those of the general population (58% in both cities).

- Average Chinese household size (3.8 in Toronto; 4 in Vancouver) is larger than the general population (2.8 in Toronto; 2.6 in Vancouver).

Table 7.4 summarizes some of the differences between the Chinese and the general populations of Toronto and Vancouver.

The same research also indicated that 57% of the household decision-makers among the Chinese population in both cities have full or part-time occupations. Toronto seems to have a higher percentage of professionals and white collar workers (27%) than Van-

## Table 7.4
## Selected Socio-economic Indicators
Base: Decision-makers in the household

|  | Canadian Population | Toronto General | Toronto Chinese | Vancouver General | Vancouver Chinese |
|---|---|---|---|---|---|
| *Gender* | | | | | |
| Male | 50% | 49% | 49% | 49% | 48% |
| Female | 50% | 51% | 51% | 51% | 52% |
| *Marital Status* | | | | | |
| Single | 24% | 26% | 36% | 26% | 37% |
| Married/cohabiting | 66% | 59% | 60% | 56% | 60% |
| Others | 10% | 15% | 3% | 18% | 4% |
| *Education* | | | | | |
| High school or below | 54% | 52% | 41% | 48% | 44% |
| College/university or above | 46% | 48% | 59% | 52% | 56% |

*Source: DJC Research 1993-1995*

couver (20%), while Vancouver has a higher percentage of home-makers (16%) than Toronto (12%). The average household income of Chinese Canadians in both cities is slightly less than $46,000. However, since many Chinese Canadians have already accumulated a significant amount of wealth before they came to this country, household income is not always a relevant measure of spending power. For example, even though Chinese Canadians in both cities have similar average income, 77% of the Vancouver Chinese live in single detached houses while 47% of the Toronto Chinese do.

## Languages

Contrary to popular belief, most Chinese people in Canada can speak English. Even so, being able to speak English does not mean they are fluent, or that they like to do business in English. Part III of this book will explore the issue of language and communication in greater detail. This section will concentrate only on the numbers:

- 70% of the Chinese in Vancouver and 65% in Toronto reported finding English "very easy" to "quite easy".
- More people from Hong Kong (74%) find English easy compared to those from China (41%) and Taiwan (51%).
- Most people from Hong Kong speak Cantonese (99%). About half of them (49%) can also communicate in Mandarin.
- Most people from Taiwan (99%) and China (91%) speak Mandarin. Only 22% of those from Taiwan can comprehend Cantonese while 73% of those from China do.
- In both cities, there are more Cantonese speaking Chinese

(77% in Vancouver; 81% in Toronto) than Mandarin speaking (63% in Vancouver; 57% in Toronto). Note that the sum of the percentages exceeds 100% because a significant percentage of the population can manage both dialects.

- 78% of those who have been in Canada for less than 5 years prefer to receive bilingual (English and Chinese) sales information. This percentage drops to 69% after 5 years, and to 63% after 10 years. The preference for Chinese in consumer activities is especially noticeable among Chinese people over 45 years of age.

## *Attitude and preference*

DJC Research measured the attitudes and preference of over 1,000 Chinese household decision-makers concerning their lives in Canada. Respondents were asked to what extent they agreed with each of the 14 statements in the survey. Findings of their research indicate that:

- Most Chinese like to try new things, especially the younger population (85%).
- Approximately half of the people will buy advertised products.
- Slightly less than half of the people under 44 may start a new business in the next two years.
- Only a third of the people find it difficult to integrate into the general Canadian society.

With respect to Chinese traditions, linkage with their last place of permanent residency, and language of preference in consumer activities, the same survey also found that the majority of the Chinese prefer to:

156

- Maintain Chinese traditions.
- Maintain close connections with friends and relatives in and receive news from their last place of permanent residence.
- Be involved in Chinese community causes and activities.
- Receive bilingual sales literature, do shopping in Chinese and be served by a Chinese-speaking salesperson.
- Like signs in Chinese where they shop, or prefer advertisement in Chinese.

## Other available information

In addition to the information in the previous sections, DJC Research also completed another extensive survey covering several thousand Chinese respondents in 1995. Based on this survey, the following information is available from DJC Research directly:

- *Media habits:* including daily/weekly/monthly reach, daypart reach, readership and sections read, channel/station/ newspaper preference, programs watched, wish list, advertisement viewing habits, VCR usage, language preference, etc.
- *Shopping habits:* including usage of different shopping aids, frequency of visits and total expenditure by store type, etc.
- *Product ownership:* including ownership and intention to own appliances, computers and communication equipment, luxury items, etc.
- *Service requirements:* including incidence, frequency of visits/use and expenditure for photo finishing, restaurants, video rental, fitness clubs, car rentals, long distance calling, gas station and auto repairs, etc.
- *Leisure and sporting activities:* including incidence, frequency of attending, watching and participating various art, enter-

tainment, and sporting activities and events.

- *Tobacco and beverage consumption:* including frequency of consumption for soft drinks, beer, liquor and wine, and cigarettes by type and brand.

- *Travel:* including incidence, frequency, purpose, services used of local and overseas travels by land and air.

- *Big ticket items:* including real estate company preference, media used relating to home purchase, type of vehicle driven/owned, financing requirements, purchase intention, etc.

- *Financial and insurance:* including banking institutions used, usage of financial services, brokerage, mutual fund companies, banking machines, credit cards, telephone banking, life insurance used by companies and types of products.

Other types of information, especially those relating to population demographics, are available from your local Statistics Canada office, Trade and Development Councils, immigration office and organizations such as the United Chinese Community Enrichment Services Society (S.U.C.C.E.S.S.) Marketing information, especially customer information, may also be available from other marketing research companies.

## Numbers, Numbers, Numbers

Mr. Tung Chan's desk shows the sign of a very neat and busy man. On the desk was a laptop computer, a four-inch pile of paperwork and a stack of reports. As a vice-president of the Toronto-Dominion Bank, Chan championed the setting up of the Asian banking group. Customers can now receive comprehensive banking services in the Chinese language through many of its branches. Banking services in other Asian languages such as Japanese, Korean, Punjabi and Hindi are also available in selected branches in the Lower Mainland. The move was greatly applauded by the bank's many Asian customers.

"This," said Chan, holding up a report from B.C. Stats, "was the reason for setting up the Asian banking group. There are almost a quarter of a million Chinese people in the Greater Vancouver Regional District alone, and the number is growing by about 2,000 a month. The business in our Chinatown offices, both in Vancouver and Toronto, is on the rise. We see trends of people and money coming our way from Taiwan and Hong Kong. So a few years ago, we made a corporate decision to set up the Asian banking group."

"We have a few guidelines to follow," Chan explained. "For example, we decided to design our products to meet the needs of new immigrants, that's why immigration and demographic numbers are so important to us. We found new immigrants want an all encompassing service, not just banking service. So we put people who can speak the customers' language in the mutual fund group, treasury group, trust service and discount and full service brokerage.

"The numbers also tell us in which branches we should put more Chinese-speaking employees. For example, 34 percent of the population in Richmond is Chinese. So we appointed Chinese-speaking managers in two of our branches in Richmond," Chan said.

Chan said at first some long-term customers were uneasy about the changes, but the results speak for themselves. The amount of business in all these Chinese-speaking or bilingual branches went up. Chinese customers found the atmosphere a lot warmer, and most customers received the change with open arms.

Chan suggested that top managers must have a vision and be open to change. They must be willing to drop past practice if that is what it takes to serve the customers.

---

After the interview with Mr. Chan, I went downstairs to a restaurant. While waiting for the meal, I went to a nearby newsstand to pick up a newspaper. The newsstand had two English dailies, two Chinese dailies and a number of community papers. I asked the news vendor, a gentleman with a Hungarian accent, how the Chinese papers were selling.

"Very well indeed, and they are getting more and more popular," he said. "Maybe it is because this mall has a lot of Chinese visitors, almost 1 in 7. And for every 10 Chinese customers, seven or eight will buy either *Ming Pao* or *Sing Tao*, two or three will buy The Sun or Province, and two or three will buy both a Chinese and an English paper."

I picked up a copy of *Business in Vancouver*, and saw an article on "Market Survey of Vancouver Chinese." Some of the numbers in the article about Chinese consumers were:

- 77 percent paid cash for the car they drive most frequently.
- 67 percent play the lottery.
- 55 percent use a karaoke machine at home.
- 18 percent spend more than $100 a week eating at Chinese restaurants.
- 3 percent spend more than $100 a week eating at "Western" restaurants.
- 11 percent spent $1,000 or more on clothing in the past year.
- 18 percent have visited a casino.
- 13 percent are skiers.
- 74 percent do not drink beer.

The list went on. My meal arrived. I was hungry and the dish looked delicious. It was time to put away the newspaper and all the numbers.

---

[1] In 1978, China decided to experiment with market economy on a limited basis. Private ownership was permitted. Special Economic Zones were designated to encourage foreign investments.

[2] As reported by Statistics Canada.

A store owner (lower right) is planning for the upcoming opening of her new store, located on an older corner of Hong Kong.
(Photo courtesy of David Au)

# Chapter Eight

# *P*lanning to Reach Your Customers

## *Introduction*

There is a general saying: "If you fail to plan, you plan to fail." This saying is true for most things in life, and is certainly true when it comes to reaching your customers, Chinese or not. Any firm that has been involved in marketing their products or services to any major customer group recognizes that success requires a great deal of careful front-end planning, constant information seeking and expert coordination of resources.

Planning is particularly important when it comes to meeting the needs of Chinese customers. As pointed out in the beginning of this book, the Chinese population in North America is a population in transition. The characteristics of this population are changing every day due to the influx of new immigrants. Their needs are also changing as they progress through the cycle of adjustment. Firms intending to meet the changing needs of a changing population will require a strategy that is both dynamic and responsive. The only way to formulate such a strategy is to constantly probe, plan and listen to your customers.

This chapter describes the planning process and some of the

factors to consider when deciding how to reach your Chinese customers. Specifically it will address the following questions:

- Should the planning be done on a corporate or department level?
- What is the focal point of the planning?
- Who should be involved in the planning process?
- What are some of the factors to consider before formulating a strategy?
- What are some of the frequently overlooked components?

There is no absolute answer to any of these questions. All firms are different, each has its own set of values and constraints. What works well for one firm may not work for another. The information in this chapter should only be used as a general guideline for your firm's planning. To what extent you should apply these guidelines will depend on your corporate chemistry.

## Total corporate involvement

A mistake many firms make when they try to reach out to Chinese customers is to consider the task as a mere marketing or sales function. As such they assign the planning and implementation to marketing or sales without allocating other resources to support their initiatives. Some even assign the task to an external marketing firm without getting directly involved. The results are often half-baked. One would-be customer's response illustrates an all-too-typical situation:

> "I saw a big ad in *Sing Tao* (a Chinese newspaper) about a furniture sale at this store. I have just

landed and bought this house and I need all kinds of furniture. The pictures in the ad are very attractive, showing a nice leather sofa, exactly what I'm looking for. So I picked up the phone to ask for directions to get there. The ad was in Chinese and I assumed I would be speaking to someone who can understand Chinese, or at least they would pass me to someone who can. You see, I'm new here and my English is not that good. I can manage a simple conversation if they speak slowly enough. But this lady who answered the phone was just too fast for me, and she said the only one who can speak Chinese is "tired" (she probably said "tied up") and can't take my call. Who do they think I am? No money to pay? I ended up going somewhere else."

Whereas good marketing is an important component in reaching the Chinese customers, it is not the only component. Reaching out to any customer group often requires a concerted effort from everyone in the firm. This is especially so when the customer group speaks a different language and belongs to a different culture. Getting a concerted effort from everyone in the firm means total corporate involvement from planning to implementation.

## Customer-driven planning

The tendency to assign an initiative to a particular department is an understandable mistake. Many firms in North America are product-driven and design their organizational structure around products instead of customers. Typically for such an organization, planning started with an existing organizational chart, and tasks were assigned to various departments without giving much thought to whether or not the firm can quickly react to shifts in customers' demands. The traditional North American planning process poses questions in this sequence:

1. Who will have need for our products?
2. How can we best position and package our products to our buyers?
3. Who will take care of production and marketing?
4. How can we monitor progress?

Such an approach to planning worked very well in the industrial era when production efficiency was the determining factor of a firm's profitability, and when the customer base was relatively stable and homogeneous. Over the last two decades, however, four major changes have had profound effects on a firm's profitability and even survivability. They are:

- Computer and telecommunication technology
- Globalization of supply and demand
- Aging of the baby boomers
- Influx of new immigrants

Most North American firms are reasonably prepared for the first three factors because these changes have been well researched and publicized. Many, however, are at a loss when it comes to reacting to the latest influx of immigrants, probably because the change was somewhat unexpected, and its effects are usually localized in major metropolitan centres. The unexpected and localized nature of the last change led many executives to underestimate its true impact until it is almost too late. Moreover, having to deal with a myriad of cultures foreign to most corporate executives adds fear of the unknown to the anxiety of being caught off-guard.

The combined effect of these four changes is an increasingly competitive market with a customer population that is well-informed, diversified and changing. A firm can no longer rely only on traditional customer loyalty for survival. To survive, a firm not only has to respond to changes in customers' needs but has to do so quickly. Product-driven planning is grossly inadequate to cope with the changing consumer demands in today's market. To adapt to these changes, and especially to the change due to the influx of new immigrants, planning must be customer-driven. As businessman Alan deGenova put it: "Do not force the customers to adopt your product. Understand the needs of the people, and develop the product to meet their needs." In customer-driven planning, questions are asked in this sequence:

1. Who are my customers and what are their needs?
2. What strategies should be used to supply my customers with what they want?
3. What are the processes involved to implement these strategies and measure feedback?
4. What are the resources required to support these processes?
5. What is the appropriate organizational structure required to coordinate these resources?

Customer-driven planning is not a revolutionary concept. To a certain extent, most traditional corporate planning is customer-driven since no firm in a competitive environment can survive without taking customers' needs into consideration. The difference here is in whether a firm views itself as a machine that processes orders or as a pool of resources to meet customers' requirements. In a market where a large number of customers have different needs because they belong to a different culture, to simply operate as an order-processing machine is to commit corporate suicide. For a firm that does not make a fundamental change in its corporate planning philosophy, no amount of ethnic window-dressing can save it from this predictable disaster.

## *The planning committee*

The planning committee responsible for reaching your new group of customers should have the following people:

- Chief Executive Officer.
- Executives in marketing, sales, customer service and human resources.
- Some front-line employees, especially those in sales and customer service.
- A business consultant with cultural knowledge.
- One or more community representatives.
- Appropriate stakeholders such as key dealers, suppliers, and/or sales agents.
- A skilled facilitator.

While the executives will eventually craft the strategies, the front-line employees and other stakeholders are just as important in the planning process. The participation of front-line people can give the executives a viewpoint from those who have direct contact with the customers. It is important to reassure them they may speak freely, without fear of retribution. Failure to do so will only make employees say what they think the executives want to hear.

Contribution from other stakeholders can help decision-makers assess the impact of their strategies. Firms concerned about confidentiality may hold a separate meeting with these stakeholders to gather their opinions without involving them directly in the planning process.

It is important to select a consultant who is familiar with both the cultural and business aspects of the industry. More specifically, this consultant should be familiar with the sub-cultures of new Chinese immigrants. He should also be objective and well-connected within the customers' community.

The role of the facilitator is to act as a gatekeeper of the planning process. This person can be internal or external to the firm, and does not have a major stake at the outcome of the planning.

The planning may take a number of day-long sessions. During these sessions, it is important for the participants to clear their minds of the pressures of their everyday work and think on a strategic level. A meeting room away from the participants' normal workplace would be most appropriate.

## Things to consider

The planning committee is ultimately interested in finding answers to these two questions:

- Should the firm pursue (or continue to pursue) Chinese customers?

- If the answer to the first question is positive, what strategy should the firm use to pursue this customer group?

This section will discuss some of the things a firm may consider before coming to an answer for the first question. In Chapter Nine, you will see examples of strategies used by some successful firms, which may assist you in finding answers to the second question.

Deciding whether or not to pursue the Chinese customer group is not at all different from deciding whether your firm should enter any other new market. A number of planning techniques can be used. None of them is, or needs to be, specific to addressing Chinese customers. A commonly used technique that can provide a quick overview of its strategic situation is SWOT analysis, which stands for strengths, weaknesses, opportunities and threats.

In SWOT analysis, a firm examines the opportunities and threats in the external environment (in this case, as related to reaching Chinese customers), as well as the firm's own strengths and weaknesses. Its purpose is to identify areas of strength the firm can draw on, and areas of weakness the firm needs to overcome, in order to pursue the opportunities and avoid the threats. Results of the analysis may indicate the firm is well-positioned to pursue this customer group, or it may show that it does not have the capability to be competitive in this market segment. In applying SWOT analysis to reaching the Chinese market segment, it is often easy to overestimate the opportunities and underestimate the threats. A firm may overestimate the opportunities because:

- Executives may react emotionally to news reports about the wealth and numbers of Chinese immigrants.
- Immigrants arrive in waves instead of a steady stream, making it difficult to do realistic projections.
- Marketing information may not be complete or available.
- The firm may not be in an industry that addresses the newcomers' needs at their stage of social adjustment.

It is equally easy to underestimate threats because:

- It is very difficult to know how many of your competitors are also planning to enter this market segment.
- Unforeseen competition may come from the new immigrants themselves, many of whom are experienced business people and have connections with low-cost foreign suppliers.
- You may have underestimated the new immigrants' preference for a competitor's brand or a substitute product.
- You may have underestimated the bargaining power of your customer group.

In assessing your firm's strengths and weaknesses, it is important to limit your analysis to areas that are relevant to your customer group. It is also important to face the issue of corporate culture head on at this time. Often executives have a tendency to list only tangible strengths and weaknesses of the firm but fail to address the less tangible issues such as corporate culture. It is embarrassing to admit, for example, that the employees in one's own firm are reluctant to embrace change, or that certain employees may have an attitude problem when it comes to serving ethnic immigrants. On the other hand, difficult as it may be, unless a firm is willing to face issues of their corporate culture upfront, any initiatives from the top may only be met with passive resistance.

Once the firm has examined its strengths and weaknesses *vis-à-vis* the external opportunities and threats, it can start to formulate strategies to capture the opportunities and avoid the threats. Often the strategies will involve riding on one's own strengths and overcoming one's own weaknesses. This is the point when many firms will assess the costs required to implement the strategies and the revenue potential of the endeavour.

In assessing costs, most firms will include some obvious cost elements such as marketing research, advertisement, employee procurement, increased staffing salaries, increased office expenses and so on. An important cost that is often neglected or underestimated is staff training. Many executives may have assumed that people should not be hired unless they already know what to do, and that most knowledge at work can be absorbed by osmosis. While true to some extent, these assumptions are not valid when it comes to reaching your ethnic customers. At least two types of training should be included into your cost estimates:

- If new employees are to be hired, they are probably hired partly because they can speak Chinese. These new employees may require training on (a) the jobs you want them to perform; and (b) North American business culture and practices.
- Existing employees who do not have the language capabilities will require training on (a) providing a responsive service to Chinese customers across cultural and language differences; and (b) working in harmony with new Chinese employees.

Experience from some firms who have launched programs to reach Chinese customers shows that most new Chinese-speaking employees are already quite familiar with the Western business practices and have little difficulty learning the job-related tasks. Nevertheless, due to deep-rooted cultural influences, these employees are less direct in their communication and tend to congregate among themselves. In addition, due to their language capabilities, they can attract more Chinese customers than other employees. In many cases, these new Chinese employees are also much better educated than their positions require and have the personality typical of the over-achievers. (You are choosing from what is probably the elite group of the population because of the immigration selection process.) Often they are able to climb the corporate ladder quickly because of their dedication and work performance.

The success of the new employees, compounded with their different communication styles and social groupings, is sometimes a source of disharmony in the workplace. Such feelings are generally not verbalized because it is politically unwise to do so, but the tension can be felt by everyone in the workplace. A good part of this type of conflict can be avoided or minimized if programs are planned upfront to facilitate workplace harmony.

## Sweating a SWOT

I was invited to take part in the strategic planning process of a company after its executive team decided to explore the possibility of making a major thrust into the Chinese market segment. Since the company is a major supplier in its industry, any reference to the type of product it provides will expose its identity. For purposes of confidentiality, I will refer to the company as Firm X, and the product they are trying to promote as Product P. The process used was SWOT analysis.

Present were the chief executive officer, the vice-presidents of sales, marketing, customer service, human resources, as well as three directors, two dealers, a facilitator and myself. I was invited to contribute my knowledge about Chinese immigrants. The two dealers were there to share the experience they have with the customers.

The facilitator briefly described the rules of the exercise:

- Say what is on your mind.
- Do not evaluate what other people say.
- Feelings are facts.

The group first discussed opportunities. Everyone took turns describing an opportunity he perceived with regard to selling Product P to Chinese consumers. The discussion went around the table again and again until no one had anything more to add. The facilitator recorded each comment on a flipchart. When the group had exhausted all thoughts on opportunities, they turned to threats, then strengths and finally weaknesses.

The meeting generated about 10 to 20 statements in each category. At that point, participants were given 20 self-adhesive red dots. The idea was for each participant to place a dot in front of any statement he felt was especially important. Each person could select no more than five statements from each category. From the exercise, the facilitator identified all the statements that had eight dots or more. Here are some from the short list:

*Opportunities*

- The Chinese population is growing by 12% a year.
- Survey indicated 60% of those (Chinese) not using Product P want to use the product within the next two years.
- 43% of the Chinese use Product P as compared to 32% of the general population.
- The Chinese inhabitants are not happy with Competitor C.

*Threats*

- Competitor C already has a first move advantage into the market.
- High probability that Firm Y will also get into the market within the next 12 months.
- Possibility that the Chinese entrepreneurs themselves will set up a firm to supply Product P.

*Strengths*

- Firm X is a highly reputable company.

- Firm X is recognized as a supplier of quality Product P in the mainstream market.
- Firm X has an efficient system to collect customers' feedback.

*Weaknesses:*

- Less than 5% of the salespeople speak Chinese.
- Less than 1% of the customer service staff speak Chinese.
- Most employees may not understand the reasons behind ethnic marketing.
- Approximately 20% of the employees may have an attitude problem when it comes to serving Chinese customers.

It was the consensus of the participants that the opportunities were certainly worth pursuing. At that point we agreed to adjourn and meet again on a future day to develop some strategies. Before we left, the facilitator wrote down two questions to channel our thoughts for the next meeting:

- How can we (a) utilize our strengths and (b) circumvent our weaknesses in order to pursue the opportunities?
- How can we (a) develop our strengths and (b) overcome our weaknesses in order to counteract the threats?

In the subsequent meeting, Firm X decided that the potential growth of the Chinese population is large enough to justify launching into this market segment. The planning committee felt that the firm has sufficient strength to become a major supplier in this market segment in spite of the threats from its competitors. Nevertheless, since it has lost the first move advantage to competitor C, it will concentrate on increasing its market share instead of profit margin in the first few years. The firm also needs to overcome its major weaknesses. Among the suggested strategies are:

- To enlist more Asian dealers.
- To provide Chinese-speaking customers with bilingual (English and Chinese) correspondence.
- To employ a number of bilingual representatives at customer service and sales.
- To train all employees in sales and customer service on providing a culturally responsive service to ethnic customers.

More about strategies will be discussed in the next chapter.

## A Growing Demand for Cross-cultural Training

Rhonda Margolis is a leading expert on cross-cultural training. For the past ten years, she has provided training to hundreds of employees in various industries, including banks and credit unions, insurance companies, post-secondary institutions, the retail industry, government and social agencies. I interviewed Rhonda to get an understanding of the new trends in cross-cultural training.

Author:     Rhonda, you started in this field at a time when almost nobody else thought it was important. Why did you pick cross-cultural training as your career?

**Rhonda:** Mainly because of my own cultural background. I am partly East Indian and partly Jewish. The diversity of my own cultural heritage sparked my interest in cross-cultural issues. After a number of years working in business, I took a degree in cross-cultural counselling and began offering cross-cultural training.

**Author:** Has the business community always been this enthusiastic about cross-cultural training?

**Rhonda:** No. When I started in 1986, I could hardly give away the training. I had to work very hard to create an interest. Now, cross-cultural training makes up 80 to 90% of what I do. There has really been a dramatic shift in interest in this area.

**Author:** What do you think is the main reason for the change?

**Rhonda:** Population change, tougher competition, and the realization that attention to language and cultural differences can have a significant impact on revenue.

**Author:** How do you see cross-cultural training fitting in with generating revenue?

**Rhonda:** Providing cross-cultural training at all levels of the organization to support the company's overall plan for attracting and keeping both customers and employees from diverse cultural backgrounds.

**Author:** What other trends do you see happening in the cross-cultural field?

**Rhonda:** There is a definite trend toward ethno-specific marketing and culturally responsive customer service. Corporate leaders recognize that it is good business to meet the needs of the changing marketplace.

Speaking the language of your customers is good business strategy. Staff at this branch of the VanCity Credit Union speak 11 languages or dialects.
(Photo courtesy of Robert Cheng)

# Chapter Nine

# *S*trategies to Reach Your Customers

Once your firm has decided to enter the Chinese market segment, the natural question to follow is: "What strategies should be used to reach these customers?" Again there is no absolute answer to this question, since much of it depends on the chemistry of your firm. This chapter will describe the strategies used by a number of firms that have been successful in this market segment.

None of the strategies used was invented solely for the Chinese customers. Instead, they are simply good applications of four basic business principles. To reach your customers, you will need to implement all four:

- Offer products that exceed your customers' expectations.
- Make it easy for your customers to know about your products.
- Make it easy for your customers to do business with you.
- Earn your customers' trust and respect.

In implementing these principles and strategies, most firms will assign a champion who is both well-connected within the Chinese community, and who has enough influence within your organization to get things done.

Throughout this chapter, I have included comments from a number of salespeople and managers. These comments represent their opinions of the lifestyles of the customers they serve. No statistical studies have been done to find out to what extent these comments can be applied to the rest of the Chinese population.

## *Offer products that exceed your customers' expectations*

In order to exceed your customers' expectations, you will need to know what their expectations are. The good news is their expectations are not difficult to discover. Most of the time you can ask, or deduce from their lifestyles. Here are some examples of how some firms determine their Chinese customers' expectations.

### From a furniture retail store

"If they like something, they'll literally sit on it. They like leather furniture, with a modern look and sleek design. They don't particularly like chestnut dining sets. I don't know why. Once you find out the styles they like, you can't put enough of them on the floor."

### From the automobile retail industry

"Why do so many of them drive Mercedes and BMWs? Obviously status has something to do with it. But my customers told me cars are so expensive in Hong Kong because of tax that luxury cars are really a deal here."

"Volvos are their favourites, probably because of its image

as a safe family car. There is a good demand for vans too, those equipped with three rows of seats. Many of my customers have large families and vans are the only type that can seat the entire family."

"We sell a lot of Hondas. Once a month we organize a special sale. We call it the '*yau-mo-gow-chor*' sale (a Cantonese phrase that means "is it for real?") when we give out very special deals. We also have an after-sale gathering with our customers. In there we show them how to maintain their cars such as changing engine oil, and they enjoy taking part in it, especially the ladies. It's like a carnival."

## From the home building industry

"We talk to the salespeople a lot and listen to our customers. There are some ethnic preferences but even the Chinese themselves don't like you to overdo them. Just avoid some obvious mistakes and you'll be all right. We sometimes consult *fēng shuǐ* masters for that reason. But the more important thing is good taste and good floor plans. You visit some Chinese friends to get a feel on how they arrange their furniture, understand their family needs and lifestyles, and avoid those plans that don't meet their needs."

"Chinese people do a lot of cooking with the wok, which means they prefer using very high power (fume) hoods. Better still, if you have a separate little kitchenette just to handle stir-frying so that the homemaker does not have to clean up the entire kitchen, that will be a plus."

"They like eight-foot doors and large entrance foyers with tall ceilings, but then who doesn't? Many of the things the Chinese like are actually very similar to what every other customer likes. They (Chinese) are very well-informed about the latest trends in finishing and layouts, probably because they see a lot of houses before they buy."

Once you find out what is important to your customers, you can then find ways to meet and exceed their expectations, such as:

- Becoming a price leader.
- Differentiating your product.
- Including additional value to your merchandise, like longer warranties, complimentary service, extra supplies or refills, etc.
- Providing exceptional service.

Which strategies you adopt depend on your competition, price elasticity, company image and profit margin. Nevertheless, whether you want to become a price leader or a supplier of added values, you can always benefit from providing exceptional service. Some other factors that are true for many Chinese customers which you may also consider before you select your strategies:

- They are knowledgeable customers. They shop around both for price and quality before they make their purchasing decisions. This is especially true for medium to large-ticket items.
- Once they find a good deal, they will tell all their friends and keep coming back to you (that is, of course, for as long as your deal is still good).
- They like good brands, and are willing to pay more for them. A good deal is a good brand product available at a discount.
- They would rather pay cash for an item than to take out a loan and incur the interest. They will see it as a deal if you

can offer a discount for cash payment.

- They are very familiar with bargaining, although at times they may choose not to practise the skill.

- If you are including added value to your merchandise, be sure that those additionals are really valuable to your customers. Otherwise, it is better to eliminate the additionals and offer a price discount. Remember that what is valuable to your mainstream customers may not be valuable to your Chinese customers.


## *Make it easy for your customers to know about your product*

We all listen to messages that get our attention, address our concerns and use a language we can understand. We also have our own "roadmaps of the world" which psychologists call "our paradigms." To make it easy for your customers to know about your products, you must get their attention, address their concerns, speak their language, and understand their paradigms. To do all these, you must understand their culture. This does not mean you need to study their art, music and literature, but it does mean you need to have a basic understanding of their lifestyles, values, familiar brands, and implications of words and symbols.

### Use a familiar brand name

Consider this comment from an appliance retailer:

"We've been trying to sell this model of fridge quite unsuccessfully for months. We knew the model sells very well in Hong Kong and couldn't figure out why it doesn't move here. One day a customer asked if the brand is the same as such-and-such brand in Hong Kong because they look exactly the same. I did some investigation and sure enough it is! To this date I still don't understand why the manufacturer uses two different brand names for the same product. No wonder it is not selling. The customers are just not familiar with the brand!"

If the manufacturer had done some homework on brand names, that mistake could have been easily avoided.

Using a familiar brand name does not mean you have to name your products "The Great Wall" or "Dragon" or something else that represents China. In fact, in some cases your brand name does not have to sound Chinese at all. Parklane Homes, a reputable builder in Vancouver, does not have a Chinese trade name, but has a lot of Chinese customers. More Chinese can recognize the name IBM than its translated name in Chinese. A well-recognized brand name in English sells better than an unfamiliar brand name in Chinese.

If you do not have a brand name that is already familiar to your Chinese customers, and need to make one up, you should get professional advice from someone who knows the Chinese culture well. A good brand name is very important because it identifies the product and projects into the minds of your customers the first impression of its quality. In selling, perception is reality. Once a perception is formed, it is very difficult to change it. As Anthony Chow, director of Colorama Productions Inc., put it: "It takes a long time to change a perception."

### Translations

At times, you may need to translate a brand name or some

sales information into Chinese. Most of us know that direct translation is awkward and sometimes may even harbour unintended meanings. Consider, for example, an English sign posted in the lobby of a hotel in Japan: "Please take advantage of our cleaning maids!" The problem of introducing unintended meanings is especially common when a message is translated into Chinese because the Chinese language permits a lot of ambiguity. Often the difference of one word can alter the meaning of the entire message.

Let us look at an example from a telecommunication company, BC TEL. Thomas Leung, Director, International Market, explained the need to recreate a name for their best-selling long-distance package for their Chinese customers:

> "We have a long-distance package called Real Plus that is meant for every one of our customers, but the name was no good for our Chinese customers because the direct translation of 'Real Plus' in Chinese means 'sure increase (in fees).' We wanted a name that could address their family ties and the need to make frequent long-distance calls. So we stayed away from direct translation and adopted the Chinese saying 'One Family Across the Distance' as the name of our package."

This does not mean messages should never be translated. Certain types of messages, such as pricing information, simple directions and product features, telephone numbers and addresses, may be translated without too many undesirable consequences. More complex messages, including slogans, brand names, sales points, may best be "transcreated" professionally by someone who has a good in-depth knowledge of the customers' language and culture.

## Symbols and graphics

Symbols and graphics can be a powerful means of communication when used appropriately. However, small details in such symbols or graphics can alter their meanings completely. Take, for example, the dragon. Many people know that Chinese people see the dragon as a symbol of good fortune, strength and power. Not too many people, however, know that a dragon without scales is a "grass dragon" (a type of insect), while a dragon without a pupil is a dragon without life and spirit. Imagine trying to appeal to your Chinese customers by using the symbol of a dragon without knowing all the details, and inadvertently missing out the scales and the pupil! Small details? Perhaps.

Do not merely insert a Chinese symbol into a graphic that was otherwise designed for the North American public. Aside from the real possibility that the combination of graphic elements may not be aesthetically pleasing, such practices run into two problems: (1) The original graphic may not convey the intended message to your Chinese customers because of cultural differences in interpreting the picture or its colours. (2) The ethnic symbols you added may come across as patronizing or even stereotyping. If you do not wish to design a different graphic for the Chinese customers, simply use your original one without the ethnic symbols. Many of your Chinese customers can interpret graphics in the Western context unless you channel them to think in the Chinese context.

## Using Chinese characters

A few well-chosen and well-calligraphed Chinese characters can be both aesthetically attractive and powerfully communicative. Some firms have used Chinese characters as their company logos, brand names, or slogans very effectively. Here, however, is an area where you most definitely need professional service (unless, of course, you are a Chinese scholar and a Chinese calligrapher yourself).

If you decide to use Chinese characters in your commercial literature or important signs, do not ask one of your employees to hand-write them simply because he is Chinese. Chinese calligraphy is an art in itself. Some traditional Chinese people may consider the aesthetic appearance of one's handwriting a reflection of one's educational level. A poorly-written set of characters in corporate publications gives your customers the perception of a company lacking in quality and professionalism. Hire the service of a Chinese calligrapher, or use Chinese typesetting. Their costs are usually very reasonable.

## Do not use "Chinese fonts"

By "Chinese fonts," I am referring to the style of English letters that are written with strokes to resemble the look of some presumably Chinese brush strokes. While it is true that you can see this type of font used in many Chinese stores and restaurants, it is aimed at North American customers. Most Chinese people find this type of font difficult to read and it does not represent Chinese culture or heritage.

## Message themes

The most effective way to address your Chinese customers is to address their needs as North Americans of Chinese heritage. Find a theme that can relate to the life of a new immigrant, the process of social adjustment, cultural harmony, education, family, employment, entrepreneuring, etc. According to Sonny Wong of Hamazaki-Wong Marketing Group and a columnist in *Business in Vancouver*, your themes should "concentrate on their needs as a Chinese living in North America, not on recreating another Hong Kong or Taiwan." Build your themes around modern applications of the traditional, and Chinese solutions to North American problems (or a Chinese version of a North American solution).

## Media selection

One question suppliers often ask is: "If we want to target the Chinese customers, should we advertise in the Chinese media?" Despite risking objections from the mainstream media, my advice is: Yes, it is a lot more cost-effective to put your ads in Chinese media. Here are the reasons:

- More Chinese use Chinese media than English media.
- Most forms of Chinese media cost less than English media.
- You do not have to say in your English ad, in effect, that the ad is meant only for the Chinese audience, thereby risking alienating other readers by exclusion, or alienating Chinese readers by using stereotypical representations.

Figure 9.1 shows the reach data of various forms of Chinese and English media to Chinese Canadians in the Vancouver area in 1995.

All the rules of media selection apply when you are choosing the right form of Chinese media. You will have to compare the costs, the reach rates, and the targeted reader groups.

## Event sponsorship

Over the past years, many firms have sponsored events and festivities run by non-profit organizations or trade associations representing different sectors of the Chinese community. Through these sponsorships, they have increased their exposure and have showed the community that they care. Used wisely, sponsorship can be very effective in building a company's image in the community.

On the other hand, firms must balance their need to gain exposure with the associated costs. As more and more organizations are jumping on the bandwagon, some firms are flooded with requests for sponsorships. Some are outraged by the amounts requested by some organizations seeking sponsorship. Before com-

## Figure 9.1: Media Usage Reach Data (Vancouver, 1995)

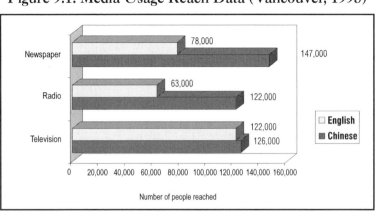

mitting your valuable dollars, ask the host organizations these questions:

- What is the specific purpose of the event?
- Who will attend the event?
- What kind of exposure will your firm have?
- How many sponsors will the host be taking?

Obviously, there is no need to agree to every sponsorship request that comes across your desk.

## Working with an advertising firm

A number of advertising firms in Canada and USA either specialize in, or have a lot of experience in advertising to the Chinese community. Before you choose one of these firms, ask for their credentials and a customer list. From the customer list you will be able to determine whether the firm has experience in a related industry, as well as in advertising to your intended audience.

Meet with the people who will actually be doing your project. As Benny Wan of the advertising firm LLT put it: "Evaluate an ethnic agency the same way you would evaluate a mainstream agency. Listen to their ideas and assess their professionalism, discipline, attitude, enthusiasm and ability to assimilate information. Look at some of the work they have done for other people and ask for successful case studies. Ask them about their ability to cope with contingencies." Once you decide to go with a particular firm, treat them as a working partner instead of a supplier. Maintain frequent communication with them until the work is complete.

## Make it easy for your customers to do business with you

You can make it easy for your customers to do business with you by:

- Taking your business to your customers.
- Offering your service in your customers' language.
- Rearranging your setting to meet your customers' needs.
- Making things simpler for your customers.

This section will discuss each of these strategies in detail and some of the associated issues:

### Take your business to your customers

One advantage of serving Chinese customers is that it is easy to find the geographic heart of their community. In most metropolitan centres, Chinese people generally live together in certain clearly identifiable localities. Moving your firm to, or opening a branch of your firm in these localities seems to be an obvious move to take. Equally obvious is that you will need people who can speak the customers' language at these branches. When opening a branch or branches at these locations, it is important to decide:

- How close should these branches be to each other before they start competing with each other for customers.
- Whether the branch will offer service in Chinese as an integral part of its overall service, or it will be segregated to specialize in providing service in Chinese.

The answer to the first question depends on population density, demographics and your firm's market share within the

Chinese community. The answer to the second question depends on your firm's business philosophy and operational efficiency. The integration approach is more conducive to assisting new immigrants in their process of social adjustment.

## Offer your service in the customers' language

More and more firms are beginning to offer multicultural service. VanCity Credit Union, for example, serves their customers in these five languages: English, French, Spanish, Cantonese and Punjabi. Most firms located in Chinese areas are beginning to see the advantage of assisting customers in Chinese. If you are a sole contributor in your business, and do not wish to hire employees, you may consider partnering with someone who can speak Chinese, preferably both Cantonese and Mandarin.

Assisting your customers in the Chinese language means, at the very least, having Chinese-speaking staff available when required. Some firms put up Chinese signs and have sales brochures and business cards available in Chinese. Others correspond with their Chinese customers in both Chinese and English, such as sending them bilingual rate guides, welcome letters and so on. Few firms, however, consider billing their customers in Chinese either necessary or cost-effective.

Note that while there are over a hundred spoken dialects in China, there is only one written language. There are, however, two versions of this written language, the traditional and the simplified. Most Chinese in Canada are more familiar with the traditional than the simplified version.

A problem associated with having Chinese-speaking staff available is that these employees may attract a disproportional number of Chinese customers. However, there are ways to minimize the uneven workload. For example, you can arrange the line-ups so that customers will be served by the first available representative regardless of language, but will be able to wait for an available Chinese-speaking representative if they so choose. Since not everyone who prefers to be served in Chinese really needs the language service, most will just go with the natural queue. Employees who cannot speak Chinese can also be trained on how to communicate with customers across a language and cultural difference (see Part III). One useful technique is to provide your employees with language cue cards in both Chinese and English, preferably illustrated, to cover the most frequently used terms and questions in your industry.

Consider, too, putting frequently requested information on video with Cantonese or Mandarin narration. Such a video can cover anything from sales information to product maintenance. Play the video in the sitting area while the customers are waiting, or hand it out as a promotional item. Since there is a large budgetary variance in video production, you will need to assess its value to you and your customers versus its cost. Generally for this kind of video, clarity and relevance of the information is much more important than its entertainment value, unless of course, you are in the entertainment business. If you do not wish to incur the expense of making a video, try at least to provide the information in print in Chinese with graphic illustrations.

The video or brochure/binder for Chinese customers does not have to have identical coverage as the material used for other customers. Sometimes Chinese customers, especially new immigrants, may have different concerns about your product. For example, while North Americans are used to wood-frame housing, most Chinese newcomers are not. If you are a home builder, you may want to elaborate certain points about wood-frame housing such as structural soundness, something you have no need to do for most other customers. To find out what your Chinese customers are concerned about in your industry, talk to them and to your salespeople.

### Rearrange your setting to meet your customers needs

Anyone on the front-line knows that Chinese customers often come in groups. Generally the group will include the entire family and either a close friend or a trusted liaison person such as their realtor. This non-family member has a fair amount of local knowledge, and serves both as consultant and interpreter. Depending on the size of the family, the group that comes to your office or store may include four to ten people. Their tendency to come in groups is partly cultural and partly the result of adjusting to a new environment.

Most North American offices or store-fronts, however, are not designed to accommodate customer groups. Front-line people often have to serve a large group in a confined space, or risk offending the customers by insisting on dealing with only one or two people. It is not always economically feasible to rearrange your office or store settings completely, so here are some suggestions for minor modifications:

- Widen a few of your service counters so that up to three

people can stand side-by-side on the customers' side. Have an open area nearby where up to six people can read or watch some information about your company or products. Explain to your customers about the space constraint at the service counter, and ask if some of the people in the group would like to, say, watch a video. Most Chinese customers will understand the need to split up the group at that time, and usually the key decision-makers and the trusted friend will come forward to the counter. Since the open area is not too far away, the two sub-groups will not feel isolated from each other, and can still consult each other if necessary.

- If your operation involves interviewing your customers in an enclosed office or cubicle, enlarge it to accommodate up to at least six people. This is especially important if your customers need to consult each other as a family during the decision-making process. Remember that an average Chinese family constitutes a couple, their children and often the husband's parents. Decisions usually made by individuals in North America may require a "family decision" in other cultures.

- Put in a few more conference rooms if space allows to accommodate more than one group at a time.

Besides the need to accommodate larger customer groups, privacy should also be a concern. While you may find Chinese customers share a good deal of information with those in their group, they do not necessarily want others to know the same information. The concern is often related to face and honour more than secrecy. Sometimes they may be sensitive to issues different from North Americans. Here are two examples:

- Whether and where one is employed (in some cases, they have not yet secured a job).

- Whether they prefer to make payments by installments.

Such questions should best be asked in a private or semi-private setting not likely to be overheard by other customers. However, you need not make a big deal out of it. For example, there is no need to conspicuously lower your voice, or to take them aside to one corner of the store.

## Make things simpler for your customers

We all know departmentalization and paperwork are two necessary evils for doing business. But there are necessary necessary evils, and there are unnecessary necessary evils. If I succeeded in confusing you with words, think of your poor customers who are confused with your processes.

No customer, Chinese or otherwise, likes to or needs to deal with more than one person in your organization for most transactions. Providing a single point of contact not only can make things simpler for them, it can make things simpler for you. For example, you may not have to hire Chinese-speaking employees in every department if your customers only need to deal with one person. Chinese customers like to build up a trusting relationship with your representatives. Sending your customers around from one department to another will not only confuse them, but will prevent them from building any long-term customer-supplier relationships with your firm.

Another way to make things simpler for your customers is to streamline both the process and format of the required paper-work, credit checking, deposit requirements, ordering and billing, waiting period, customer agreements and contract renewals. Obviously there is a place for these elements in business, but none of them should be so burdensome as to turn customers away.

You may also consider being more flexible when it comes to applying credit policy to some of your Chinese customers. Many of them may have very deep pockets, but have yet to establish a credit record with the local bureau. In addition, many new immigrants may be unemployed or under-employed although they may have a substantial net worth. If you insist on using credit record and salary income as the yardstick for measuring their credit-worthiness, you may run the risk of losing a lot of credit-worthy customers.

## Earn your customers' trust and respect

The ultimate strategy to increase your market share is to earn your customers' trust and respect. Your customers will like to do business with you if they feel that you care for them. They will trust and respect you if they know you always stand by your word. The following strategies have been used by most successful firms.

### Show your customers that you care

Most people respond in kind. When you care for your customers, they will care for you. When you care for your customers' community, the customers' community will care for you. You can show your caring for your customers' community by:

- Sponsoring community events and organizations.
- Getting involved in community issues.
- Appointing members of the community to your board.
- Having a fair representation of the community in all levels

of your operation.

- Encouraging your staff to be involved in the media and community events.
- Offering free seminars for the community.

Unlike most other business strategies, the result of your efforts here may not be immediately measurable. Often you will need to persevere without much sign of encouragement. Nevertheless, once the "incubation period" is over, the payback can be very high.

## Provide responsible customer service

Some people say the best way to tell how reliable a firm is to look at the way they treat their customers after the sale. You can only get repeat customers and customer referrals if you provide reliable and efficient service. Your customers will like your service if you:

- Always follow up on customers' complaints promptly.
- Honour all warranties, written or otherwise.
- Fix your mistakes.
- Provide a single point of contact.
- Walk the extra mile for the customer.

Once you establish yourself as a respectable and responsible supplier within a community, the people in the community will do the selling for you, free. The Chinese community is closely knit. Word of mouth is your most powerful ally in reaching your customers in this community.

## *Business Strategies of a Home Builder*

"It was the best of times, it was the worst of times." The words that Charles Dickens used to describe Paris in the late eighteenth century can be used to describe the real estate market in Greater Vancouver over the past decade. There were times when houses could not be built fast enough. There were times when some home builders went from boom to bust. Yet whether it was the best or the worst times, there were a few builders whose products have always stood the test of the market. One such company is ParkLane Homes.

On a bright morning in May 1995, I brought my lecture materials into the ParkLane Hall at Eagleridge Hospital in Coquitlam, a fully-equipped meeting room ParkLane donated to the hospital as a token of thanks to the community. ParkLane had borrowed the room for the day. Everyone here in the room, from the president to the secretaries, focused their attention on learning about their Chinese customers for the next eight hours. I was deeply moved by their sincere desire to know more about their customers, their culture and their needs. The energy in the room that day gave me the best explanation for ParkLane's reputation both within and outside of the Chinese community. A few weeks after my lecture, I interviewed ParkLane's president, Peeter Wesik, to find out the strategies behind ParkLane's continued success. Here are some excerpts from the interview:

## On meeting customers' expectations

"Part of our mission is to fulfil the customers' dreams and exceed their expectations. We place a lot of emphasis on finding out and providing what people want. We know if we give them quality, value and service, we will be further ahead in the long term."

"We learned that what our Asian customers want is not substantially different from what our other customers want. All of us want an attractive house and good quality of design. Obviously certain groups appreciate and are willing to pay for certain design more than others. The key is to find out the type of design and finish your customers want and are willing to pay for."

## On marketing and sale

"We put a lot of effort and pride in our advertisements (for which they have won many awards). We have a responsibility to tell our customers about our products."

"Where we identify a group of customers, we will always look for a promotional channel that is the most direct way to reach that customer group. This means to find out the newspapers they like to read, places they like to be, and to have promotional material available in their language."

"We recognize the importance of referred sales. We work within the existing realtor community, and form a strategic alliance with realtors."

## On customer service

"We always make sure that our customer support representatives have the language skills to communicate with our customers, to identify problems, so that they can relate the problems to our service people."

"Our customer service program has been named the best in the province for the past three years. It's very important to us, because so many of our buyers are referred to us by existing customers."

(ParkLane also offers a binder to every one of their customers, explaining the structure, components, finishing and landscaping of a typical home, along with information about the community in which the home is located. The binder is available in English, French and Chinese.)

## On goal

"Our main goal is to ensure ParkLane remains as a well-respected builder."

# Part III

# *M*eeting and Networking
# with Your Customers

*"A person who does not smile should not open a shop."*

— A traditional Chinese adage

# *I*ntroduction to Part III

When interacting with your Chinese customers, there are three key concepts to bear in mind: holistic thinking, the importance of face and the practice of *kì qì* (Cantonese: *hark hay*). These three concepts are the underlying basis of all social interactions and interpersonal relationships among Chinese people. Due to their extraordinary significance, they will be discussed first.

## *Holistic thinking*

A fundamental difference between Chinese and North American culture lies in the way people perceive things. People in North America are very good at taking things apart and looking at each piece of a puzzle independently — so good that sometimes people may forget to put the pieces back together. This is analytical thinking. In the East Asian cultures, things are rarely looked at apart from their surrounding context and implications. Everything is viewed in relation to and in conjunction with other things in the bigger picture. This is holistic thinking.

Here is an example of the difference between the two types of thinking: There are four birds sitting on a branch. If someone threw a stone and killed one of them, how many birds would be left on the branch? In analytical thinking, one would look at the problem as a simple mathematical one, and give the answer of three. In holistic thinking, one would see the implication of the stone throw, and give the answer of zero because after you killed the first bird, the others would fly away. Both types of thinking are correct, and people in both cultures use both analytical and holistic thinking. The difference is in the degree of emphasis.

This difference in the way people perceive things is manifested in many facets of social interaction, especially in communication patterns and building social relationships. In interacting with your Chinese customers, it is necessary to temporarily "empty your mind" and try to see things the way your customers do. This includes discarding the Western basis of "effective communications," and listening to your customer's message instead of merely the words. It also means putting aside the Western notion that personal relationships can be compartmentalized, that it is possible to confine one another's relationship to certain definable realms. For example, most Westerners draw a clear line between business and personal relationships, while traditional Chinese tend to blend the two relationships together.

### The importance of face

Face is perhaps the most important word to remember when meeting with your Chinese customers. It is so important that you will not go very far in the Chinese society without it or understanding how it works. An individual's face in the Chinese community is equivalent to a firm's credit rating in business.

Face, or *miàn zi* (in Cantonese: *meen tsee*), is a person's social prestige, a measure of how high a person is in society in terms of his or her wealth, power and ability to influence people. In a way, the Chinese concept of face is not a lot different from the Western concept of face, in that it refers to both the front side of a person's head and one's esteem. The difference is the degree of emphasis between the two cultures, to the extent that the Chinese have developed an unwritten set of rules governing face.

Since face is so important in the Chinese social fabric, most Chinese spend an enormous amount of effort in maintaining each other's face. Such efforts are called "face-working." In general, this "face-working" involves maintaining one's own face while not causing offence to the other person's face. Where appropriate, it also involves doing something actively to enhance another person's face.

The need to maintain one's own face is manifested in many different ways. At the very least, it involves not showing one's weak side, which can be anything from failing to comprehend sales information to not having enough cash to pay for an item. Other ways to maintain one's face may include presenting one's best side in front of others, such as wearing expensive clothing or jewellery, or insisting on paying for friends' meals at a restaurant. To those who are not familiar with how face works, this type of behaviour may sometimes come across as showing off one's wealth. The true intention, however, is often related more to face than to flaunting.

Chinese people take great precautions not to offend other people's face. To do so is equivalent to splashing a drink onto the face of the offended. In a society which values harmony above all, few people can afford to be careless in this respect. There are many ways in which a person's face can be offended. The most common way is to slight a person, whether intentionally or inadvertently. To slight a person is to imply that he or she has less face than you and deserves an inferior position in the invisible social hierarchy. Slights can come in many forms and shapes, from being subtly arrogant to outright rude. Other forms of slights include holding an aloof attitude, bluntly refusing a request, sending someone of a lower rank to receive a high-ranking guest, neglecting to receive guests at the door or to accompany them out.

To enhance each other's face, Chinese people often spend a great deal of time praising each other while effacing themselves. This type of practice sometimes makes Westerners feel uneasy and unnatural. Once you understand this is only a part of the socializing process and is a form to express humility, you will not be disturbed by what appears to be superfluous praise or other such behaviours. Other ways of enhancing a person's face include granting the person his requests, inviting the person to important functions and seeking advice from him.

Face is like a bank account or a credit card. You can use it to "buy things" (i.e. cause things to be done) but you can also overdraw your account. You can increase the balance of your face account by holding influential positions, increasing your wealth, becoming a celebrity or recognized expert, doing favours for your associates or widening your network of contacts. You can overdraw your account if you ask for too many favours without giving anything back, or if one day people find out you are not who you led them to think you are.

### The practice of *kè qì*

*Kè qì*, or in Cantonese *hark hay*, is the way a Chinese person treats a guest. It is also the unwritten behavioural code between two individuals in the initial stages of their relationship. It refers to the set of behaviours characterized by politeness, courtesy, modesty, self-effacement, understanding and consideration.

While Chinese people are used to being treated with *kè qì*, many Westerners may find the exceedingly polite treatment somewhat awkward. The proper Chinese way to respond to such polite behaviour is to match it with equally polite behaviour. For example, you may see your Chinese friend gesturing his associate to enter into a meeting room before him. The associate, in turn, may insist that your friend should have the honour of entering first. The two can keep on gesturing to each other back and forth a few times until one of them gives in. To people outside the culture, the small commotion may seem a waste of time or even appear comical. To people inside the culture, this sort of behaviour is a necessary process to avoid inadvertently upstaging one another.

Unless you have been working among Chinese people for a long period of time, it is unlikely you can match their level of *kè qì*. Your best policy is to behave the way you are, be sincere in what you do and say, and acknowledge the courtesy they show you. In most cases, your Chinese friends will understand that you do not know their code of behaviour and will not interpret your lack of reciprocation as a sign of arrogance.

## A matter of attitude

Holistic thinking, face and *kè qì* behaviour are the three key elements to bear in mind when you interact with your Chinese customers. You will certainly be at an advantage when you can think like your customers (holistic thinking), feel like your customers (face), and behave like your customers (*kè qì*).

On the other hand, your Chinese customers will know that you do not know their social behavioural codes. They will forgive you for not thinking the way they think, for not valuing face to the extent they value it and for not reciprocating some of the *kè qì* behaviours. As long as you are sincere in what you do, they will understand. Your attitude is much more important than your behaviour.

A word of caution: In my dealings with the North American public, I have found that most people are sincere, friendly and have an open attitude. There is, however, a small percentage of people from all walks of life whose attitude leaves something to be desired. These people harbour an air of superiority in the way they interact with people of other racial origins. Although they may not verbally convey their feeling of superiority, their arrogance and aloofness can be felt by anyone around. No matter how carefully these people conceal their feelings, they will always show through in subtle ways. For a group of customers who are used to reading audible as well as silent messages, hiding arrogance behind polite verbiage is as effective as covering the body with the Emperor's new clothes.

Needless to say, an attitude of racial superiority has no place in any business dealing that sees customers coming from other countries. Your customers will forgive you for not understanding their cultures or languages, but they will not forgive you for slighting them on racial grounds. Such an attitude makes poor business sense. It violates the principle of face. It violates the principle of fairness. Above all, it is wrong.

## *The next four chapters*

The next four chapters can only be understood in the context of the three key elements described in this introduction. Each chapter contains description of behaviours, manners and etiquette. While these are important behaviours to learn when interacting with your Chinese customers, your underlying attitude is incomparably more important.

Chapter Ten describes how to prepare for a meeting with your Chinese customers, things to pay attention to during a meeting, how to get your point across, how to say no, and some commonly accepted Chinese manners and business etiquette.

Chapter Eleven deals with the problem of communicating across a language difference.

Chapter Twelve discusses how you can generate interest, handle objections and resolve conflict with your Chinese customers.

Chapter Thirteen shows you ways to network with and build trust in your Chinese customers.

Your customers may come in all shapes and sizes. A group of young customers visiting a Chinese herbal store.
(Photo courtesy of Robert Cheng)

# Chapter Ten

# *M*eeting Your Customers

Most businesses require you to meet with customers at least some of the time. The business community in North America has adopted a fairly standardized etiquette regarding meetings, from what to wear to how to exchange business cards. Most Chinese customers are very familiar with North American business etiquette. However, there are some seemingly minor differences between the two business cultures. To make your customers feel at home, and to show that you respect their ways of doing things, it pays to find out how your customers' greet and discuss business with one another. This chapter will explore the following topics:

- Preparing for a business meeting
- The initial contact
- Manners
- Business talk

## *Preparing for a business meeting*

### The meeting place

You can meet your customers anywhere — at your office, a restaurant, a hotel lobby, the customer's home — depending on the nature of the business and your customer's preference. The setting can be either formal or semi-formal. There is really no

215

cultural preference as to where one should meet. When in doubt, lean toward the formal.

The meeting rooms in Taiwan and mainland China are typically furnished with three rows of single sofas or chairs arranged into the shape of a letter "U," with the door on the open side of the letter. In the middle of the wall facing the door is the seat for the host and, to its right, the seat for the guest of honour. Sitting next to them are the interpreters. Other guests and members of the host's party will sit along the two sides.

There is no need to rearrange your meeting room to resemble a Chinese setting. Most Chinese customers are very familiar with Western arrangement. Moreover, although this setting is common in Taiwan and mainland China, the standard Western setting is more commonly used in Hong Kong.

## What to wear

Unless you are meeting your customer at a country club, it is always safer to be on the formal side when it comes to clothing. In most situations, formal does not mean wearing tuxedo; your normal business attire should be sufficient.

It is possible that some of your Chinese customers may come to the meeting wearing designer clothes, diamonds and a Rolex watch. In most cases, it is their way of maintaining face since they have no idea who they may run into during the course of the day. Rightly or wrongly, in a materialistic culture such as that of Hong Kong, material possessions are sometimes used to protect one's face. Unless you are selling jewellery, there is no need to try to match your customers' diamonds or Rolexes. It is also possible

216

that some of your Chinese customers may come to you in rather shabby clothes. It is important to remember that what one wears is really not a true reflection of one's level of wealth. Many of us have met people of great influence dressed in something very ordinary. Well-dressed or not, a customer is a customer.

You will know after a while how most of your customers dress. You may then adjust your attire to reflect your customers' preferences. Most people, Chinese or not, like to deal with people similar to themselves. Always, however, be professional.

## Punctuality and pace

There is no difference between serving your Chinese customers and other customers when it comes to punctuality. The rule is: always be punctual. If you happen to be late, you need to apologize and provide an explanation. Your Chinese customers will appreciate your respect for their time.

Many of the Chinese customers, especially those from Hong Kong, are used to the rhythm of a fast-paced environment. If at all possible, try to reduce both the waiting and the transaction time. For people who have always lived in the fast lane, efficiency is the key. This does not mean you should rush your customers or reduce the amount of personal attention. It does mean, however, that you may want to change some of the processes in your organization to make them more efficient.

## The initial contact

### Greetings

Most of your Chinese customers will understand enough English to say "hello," "good morning," and "how are you?" They may not understand, however, if you say "whadaya say?" or "how ah ya?"

Learn to say one or two standard greetings in Chinese. They are not too difficult and you can break the ice with them. Even if you cannot pronounce the greetings accurately, your customers will understand you are just trying to be friendly. The best way to learn Chinese (Cantonese or Mandarin) is to take a language course. However, since you do not need a course to learn just a couple of expressions, you may consider learning them from your Chinese customers or friends. There are also language tapes available commercially. Here are the closest approximation of the greetings using the English phonetic system for Cantonese and *pīn yīn* system for Mandarin:

> *Cantonese:*
>> "*Jo sun*" means "good morning."
>> "*Lay ho ma?*" means "how are you?"
> *Mandarin:*
>> "*Zăo*" means "good morning."
>> "*Nĭ hào?*" means "how are you?"

The verbal greeting is usually accompanied by a handshake. Practically every Chinese customer is familiar with this form of greeting. It is one of the Western habits that has been widely adopted by the Chinese people, even among themselves. Unlike some other Asian cultures, the Chinese culture does not prohibit women from shaking hands. In this respect, all Western rules apply. Many Chinese people also dip their heads as they shake hands. The dipping of the head is in fact a slight bow.

Occasionally you may come across a few customers who shake your hand with both of theirs (their left hand will touch the back of your right hand) and give you a bow more than a slight dip of the head. This is a form of deep respect or sincere gratitude. Your best reaction is to respond in kind. Unlike the Japanese, Chinese people do not bow to each other in everyday greetings. Bowing is usually reserved for ceremonial functions or used as a gesture of deep respect.

A gesture Chinese people like to use sometimes is to cup their hands, raise them either to chin level or above the head, then swing the cupped hands forward a few times as if they are swinging a hammer. This is a very traditional form of Chinese greeting and is used during the festivals as a way to congratulate one another more than a form of everyday greeting.

### Entering a customer's house

It is quite possible that your meeting may take place in your customer's residence. Most Chinese people in North America will remove their shoes once they enter the host's house. The practice is based on practical reasons: it makes it easier for the hostess to clean up after you leave. Your hosts may feel uncomfortable asking you to remove your shoes, and may even ask you to keep them on. However, unless your hosts are wearing shoes themselves, it is generally more considerate to remove them. The only exception is when you know the removal of your shoes will embarrass yourself and everyone around. Generally your host will supply you with a pair of slippers. Otherwise, simply wear your socks.

Once inside, your host will usually ask if you care for a drink. A drink for most Chinese means a hot Chinese tea or a cold beverage such as juice or a pop. Unless your host specifically asks if you like to have an alcoholic beverage, do not ask for one. Many Chinese households may not even have beer or wine in stock. You can imagine the embarrassment to the host if you ask for, say a Martini. If you are served Chinese tea, do not ask for sugar or cream. Chinese tea is always served plain. Besides not a good mix, your action is telling the host that you need to mask the flavour of his tea. If you like the tea, compliment on its aroma. If you don't, do not make an issue out of it.

### Exchanging business cards

Chinese people exchange their business cards with a great deal of reverence. They usually hold the card with both hands and present it to the recipient with a slight bow. The text side of the card should be facing up, oriented in such a way that it can be read by the recipient. The recipient should also receive the card with both hands and return a slight bow. Then he should take a few seconds to read the information on the card before putting it away.

It is a good idea to follow this practice when presenting your business card to your Chinese customers to show your respect for the tradition. Moreover, the gesture itself holds a special meaning. In most Asian cultures, presenting an object with both hands implies you respect the recipient as well as value the object you are presenting. It also forces you to pay exclusive attention to the action itself since you do not have a hand free to do anything else. To Chinese business people, the business card is more than a little piece of paper. It represents them and they expect you to keep it carefully. Do not write on the face of the card, it is like writing on someone's photograph.

A problem with exchanging business cards using both hands is that it can be awkward if the cards are exchanged simultaneously. To avoid this situation, if you feel that your customer is about to present you his card, accept it first before you present your own. If you feel awkward presenting the card with both hands, you can still present it with one hand since most customers will understand this is not your custom. However, do not sandwich the card between your index and middle finger like you are holding a cigarette and push it into the direction of the recipient. Some Chinese people may interpret this gesture as obscene.

Most Chinese business people in North America use bilingual business cards, with Chinese on one side and English on the reverse. You may consider getting yourself some. Having bilingual cards will show that your company really wishes to connect with Chinese customers. It also makes it easier for your customers to remember you. In designing a bilingual card, there is no need to translate all the information into Chinese. Many Westerners will have only their names and titles translated, leaving the addresses and telephone numbers in English and numerals. There is no rule as to how much information should be translated.

Be careful, however, with the way your English name is translated. All Chinese names have meanings and, like people of other cultures, Chinese like to use well-meaning words for their names. English names are usually translated phonetically into Chinese without considering the eventual meaning of the words chosen. If not carefully done, the result could be embarrassing. Sometimes you may even end up having a name that sounds like a joke. An Irish friend of mine (named O'Reilly) once asked me to comment on his newly acquired Chinese name. I told him frankly that the translated name sounded like "getting sick from diarrhoea" in Chinese and suggested that he have it changed. A good translation should be phonetically appropriate, well-meaning and similar to a traditional Chinese name.

## Names and titles

In the Chinese naming system, family names are always put before the given names. This is the reverse of the Western naming system, and often is a source of confusion. For example, say your customer tells you her name is Ms. Chu Wai Lee. You may wonder if she is Ms. Chu or Ms. Lee. Some Chinese people adjusted to this discrepancy when they came to North America by adopting the Western system. However, this still does not solve the problem. For example, you may now have a customer called Ms. Wai Lee Chu instead of Ms. Chu Wai Lee. Is it any less confusing?

The best way to find out is to ask. When you are asking, do not use the term "last name" or "first name." Use instead "family name" and "given names." Most Chinese family names are made of a single monosyllable character, such as Chan, Lee, Cheung, Wong, Ho, etc. Given names can be a single character or two characters. Where given names are made of two characters, they will usually be joined together with a hyphen when written in English. For example, my Chinese given name is *Wai-man*, so hyphenated because it is composed of two Chinese characters "*Wai*" (meaning "magnificent") and "*Man*" (meaning "civilization" or "literature").

Many Chinese people have adopted English given names. While such names will be easier for Westerners to pronounce, the names may not constitute part of the customers' legal identity. This is important if you need the exact legal name of the customer either for registration or credit-checking purposes. A married woman may not always adopt her husband's family name in legal documents. Sometimes she keeps her original family name. Sometimes she adopts the husband's name. In many cases, she hyphenates her own name and her husband's family name.

Many English-speaking people find Chinese names difficult to pronounce, and are concerned that mispronouncing a customer's name will offend him. The fact is a Chinese name when written in English is no longer the original name. Unless you know the original language, you will only be pronouncing an Anglicized form of the name. Most Chinese people in North America are used to hearing people pronouncing their Anglicized names. As long as you follow the English phonetic system in pronouncing the names, you will not be right but they will not be offended either. Even if you are fairly off-base (for example, try to pronounce my family name, Ng!) so long as you do not follow it with a puzzled or amused expression, your customer will generally understand. If you are really not sure, ask your customer.

The problem of creating an embarrassing name during the course of translation also happens when Chinese names are translated into English. Although it does not happen often, some very embarrassing names still surface from time to time. This is because the individual who did the translation may not always have had a good understanding of English slang and other more embarrassing words. After all, these words are not taught in school.

A sales representative at a telephone company once told me about a Chinese female customer wanting a telephone line installed at home. When asked her given name, the customer gave her a four-letter word beginning with the letter 'S'. Phonetically speaking, this word is a perfect translation of an innocent Chinese word meaning snow, which is a fairly common given name for Chinese girls. Due to the connotation associated with the word in English, most Chinese females with the name Snow have adopted a different translation, *Suet*. A few people, however, are still unaware of the problem and continue to use the other version of the translation. If your customer presents you with an embarrassing name, respect that this is still the customer's name and do not show any sign of surprise or amusement. If the name needs to be printed onto a public document, try to use only the customer's initials. Fortunately, I have not come across any family name that belongs in this unprintable category.

## Meeting with a group

Since Chinese customers often come in groups, it is important to know the proper way to greet them collectively. Unless the group is very large, it is always nice to be able to greet each person one at a time. You may start in the order of proximity, and be sure not to ignore the women and the seniors. Show special respect to the senior members, such as by using both of your hands to do the handshake and giving them a slightly deeper bow (about 30 degrees is sufficient). Respecting the elderly is a virtue among the Chinese people. The seniors in Chinese families are regarded as the source of wisdom. Often they have much more influence in family decisions than their gestures suggest. By seeking their advice from time to time, you will win the hearts of young and old alike.

Generally there is a spokesperson for the group. This can be an interpreter, a trusted friend, or the decision-makers themselves. Chinese people are very used to making decisions as a group. Often you will see them talking to one another, possibly in Chinese, after talking to you. If they are using their own language, you can almost be sure that they do not mean to exclude you. They simply find it easier to converse in Chinese.

## Small talk

There is no rule on how much informal small talk should precede formal business talks. Some customers want to get to the point to save time, others like the more personal approach. Try to see if the customer is in a hurry or whether he is comfortable with small talk. The customer's gestures will tell you whether you should get right to the point. The key is to be natural and to respect the customers' needs for both personal attention and business efficiency. Formal or informal, a smile will always leave a better impression than a stern face.

If you decide to engage the customers in informal conversation, be aware of the difference in popular culture. For example, famous American sports stars may be household names in North America, but they may be complete strangers to a newcomer. Stay away from talking about local politics, not so much for political reasons, but because they will only make as much sense to your customers as the local politics in Hong Kong or Taiwan would to you. Some favourite topics to Chinese customers include: Your visits to Asia, their experience in Canada, places to see, children, etc. The perennial topic of the weather is not as commonly discussed among Chinese as it is among Westerners.

Humour is often culture-specific. What is really hilarious in one culture may not be funny at all in another. For example, British humour is quite different from American humour, even though people of the two countries speak the same language. Imagine how a pun would confuse someone who is still struggling with the language. If your customers are not laughing at your jokes, usually it is not because they lack a sense of humour.

## Smoking

You may find that a fair percentage of your Chinese customers smoke. If they are smoking in a non-smoking area or building, it is generally sufficient to explain that the area is designated as non-smoking. Show the customer where he can enjoy his smoke. Most smokers are aware of the need to restrict smoking to designated locations, and cordial reminders are generally not offensive to the customer.

If your customer smokes in a non-restricted area and you are uncomfortable with second-hand smoke, you will need to decide if you want to bear the discomfort or risk offending the customer. If the meeting is short or the customer is only an occasional smoker, it is better not to raise the issue. If the meeting is long and the customer is a frequent smoker, he probably needs the nicotine to stay awake. If you are really uncomfortable, you may apologetically explain your limitation to the customer. Most people will understand, but there is no fool-proof way not to offend some customers.

If you are a smoker, the rule is not to light up unless your customer does first. Many people may say they do not mind you smoking simply because they do not want to offend you. The majority of non-smokers do mind other people smoking around them, although they may not verbalize their objections.

## *Manners*

Chinese newcomers are often impressed by the good and friendly manners of the people in North America. Most Americans and Canadians are brought up to say "please," "thank you," and even to say "hi" to people they have never met before. Western cultures also put a lot of emphasis on table manners and proper dress codes. In general, Western manners emphasize being courteous, pleasant and elegant.

## Lǐ mào

The term for manners in Chinese is *lǐ mào*. The word *lǐ* implies a code of behaviours used in ceremonies and interpersonal affairs. A good part of Confucius' teaching was devoted to *lǐ*. In essence, for Confucius and for the Chinese people, the practice of *lǐ* is the sign of a civilized person. The word *mào* implies one's appearance. Strangely enough, Confucius did not devote nearly as much attention to *mào* as he did to *lǐ*. Thus it seems that while both behaviour and appearance are a part of the Chinese code of manners, how one behaves towards other people is far more important than how one looks. A subset of *lǐ* is the practice of *kè qì*, the code of behaviour between a host and a guest.

While Chinese people are very polite to the people they associate with, they are often indifferent to those people they regard as strangers. This is contrary to the North American practice in which people are expected to be polite to everyone. Although more and more Chinese people are seeing the advantage of being polite to everyone, you may still come across some customers who treat you like a stranger. This explains why sometimes Westerners complain that some Chinese people are very rude.

Also keep in mind that your Chinese customers come from a very diverse educational background. There are plenty of university graduates. There are also plenty of people who never had the luxury of schooling. Likewise, while there are many well-mannered Chinese people, there are also many who do not know enough English to tell "please" from "thank you," or understand the need to line up in front of a service counter.

If a Chinese customer is not following the rules everyone else is following, such as jumping the line, treat him the way you would with any other customer behaving the same way. Give him the benefit of the doubt that he genuinely mixed up the ends of the line (many indeed did, due to lack of clarity of signs or inability to read English). Courteously show him where the line begins. Do not say "In this country, we line up for our services."

## Eye contact

Westerners are brought up to think that direct eye contact is a gesture of sincerity and interest. Avoiding eye contact is often interpreted as poor manners or as a signal that the speaker has something to hide. This view of eye contact is not universal. In fact in some cultures, such as the First Nations of Canada, direct eye contact is regarded as rude or even hostile.

There is virtually no rule about eye contact for the Chinese. If there is, the rule is both inconsistent and changing. Some older people may consider it is impolite to look into people's eyes. Others do not mind, unless you are staring at them. Still others may not mind but would feel uncomfortable looking back at you because of shyness.

Traditionally, Chinese people do not look into each other's eyes when they talk to one another. Many people, however, are exposed to enough Western culture to recognize the importance of eye contact. Your best policy is to take the lead from your customers. If they feel comfortable with eye contact, look them in the eye. If they look elsewhere while talking with you, look at the paperwork or the merchandise. In any case, do not be offended.

## Business talk

Whether you start off with small talk or get right down to work, here are some points to bear in mind when talking business with your Chinese customers:

*Be sincere.* There is nothing more important than to be sincere when doing business with Chinese customers. Historically, Chinese people have a great deal of mistrust for business people. Although this attitude is quickly changing, many Chinese customers still reserve a certain degree of scepticism when dealing with the business world. For this reason, most Chinese people prefer to do business only with those in their connection network. They will also back away from any deal as soon as they detect the slightest sign of insincerity.

*Know your product well.* Your customers expect you to know a great deal about your product because this is the way business is conducted in Asia. Not too many customers will have the patience to wait for you to check out product information from literature or with your boss. Once they find out that you have the required product knowledge, you can earn their trust easily and they will come back to you as an expert in your field.

*Be precise in your description.* Say 1,850 square feet, or 2.8 litres, or 5-year warranty. Do not say about 2,000 square feet, about 3 litres, or a long warranty period, unless the measured quantity is irrelevant to the point of discussion. This is especially important when the commodity is scarce in the customer's place of origin. For example, the difference between 1,850 square feet and 2,000 square feet of space can be very significant if they had been paying $500 per square foot!

***Be mindful of your customer's comprehension level.*** You will know within the first few minutes of your meeting the customer's comprehension level in English. Adjust your talking speed, choice of vocabulary and expressions accordingly. However, do not assume that all your Chinese customers will have difficulty communicating in English. Many Chinese newcomers speak English very well. Adjusting your pace or vocabulary inappropriately would come across as patronizing.

***Use terms that are familiar to your customers.*** Regardless of English skill, always choose terms that are familiar to your customers. For example, Chinese customers are used to seeing discount information expressed as the percentage they will eventually pay rather than the percentage taken off the price. Thus instead of saying 10% off, say pay 90% of the price. Find out from your customers what other terms you may need to change in your industry.

***Listen to clues and silent messages.*** This is perhaps the most difficult part for Westerners when communicating with Chinese people. Clues are generally easy to pick up if you are alert. Silent messages are a different ball game. For those readers who have difficulty understanding how messages can be in silent form, think of the rest notes in a piece of music. A rest note is not an omission but a strategically placed silence to enhance the musical value of the piece. Chinese people communicate with both words and pauses. Pauses sometimes convey messages just as powerful as words but a lot less destructive. If you detect an unnatural silence on the part of your customers, think back on what you have just said before the pause. Your customer is either waiting for more information or having reservations about what he has just heard. Alternatively, your customer may have something to tell you but hesitate to do so because he is not sure of how you would react. Try to guess what your customer may be up to from the context of the conversation and skillfully provide a clue regarding your position on the matter.

**Be mindful of your customer's face.** This is crucially important. There are two points in the course of a business transaction when it is particularly easy to cause someone to lose face. One is when you are informing the customer about your product. There is often just a fine line between informing and patronizing. When you cross that line, you will cause the customer to lose face. Often the difference is in the tone or the way you explain something. The other is during the course of negotiation. Try to leave something on the plate for everyone and do not negotiate to the last dime. Some customers may stop negotiating just because you have put them into a position where they would lose face no matter what they do.

**Be tactful when you have to say "no."** Many Chinese people regard a flat "no" as a slap on the face. Among the Chinese, they often say "it is inconvenient" or "let me consider it" instead of "no." In Chinese, everyone knows such expressions are merely tactful ways of saying "no", yet in English they do not carry the same connotations. In English "it is inconvenient" means exactly that, and "let me consider it" means you do not have an answer yet but in time you will have one. To avoid possible misunderstanding, do not just say "let me consider it." If you mean you will consider the request, say "let me consider it and get back to you by such and such time." And if you mean to say "no," follow these three steps:

- Acknowledge the customer's request and the reasons for it.
- Explain the difficulties involved in granting the request.
- Offer an alternative, even if it is not a substitute.

## *You Don't Have to be Chinese to Sell to the Chinese*

Everyone who has some knowledge of the real estate market in the Greater Vancouver area knows the area has two distinct market segments: local buyers and off-shore/immigrant buyers. One of the top marketers who does very well in both market segments is Bob Rennie of Ulinder Project Marketing Corporation. Bob is Caucasian and he does not speak Chinese.

I had the privilege of meeting Bob at his office in downtown Vancouver. In spite of his very busy schedule, Bob was prompt to the minute. He shook my hand with enthusiasm, presented his business card with both hands, and gestured me to enter the board room before him. His *kè qì* behaviour came so naturally and so sincerely, I wondered where he learned it from.

Not to waste any of his time, I was all ready to start the interview. Bob, however, engaged me in a brief chat first. He told me he was born and raised in Vancouver. Throughout the years, he saw how much the city has benefited from the influx of immigrants from around the world. Here are some of Bob Rennie's thoughts on marketing to off-shore buyers:

### On treating off-shore customers

"I find the wants and desires of immigrants are no different from local buyers. They need schools, buses, shopping, standard lot size, just like anyone of us. They will buy exactly what the local market wants, and those devel-

234

opers who build exclusively for the off-shore market will find that their products are not salable."

"Any attempt to use a two-tier pricing strategy, one for local buyers and one for off-shore buyers, simply does not work."

## On providing product information

"People need to make informed decisions, whether they are local, new immigrants or off-shore. New immigrants need to have all available information just like locals. If the information presented to them is not complete or precise, they will become sceptical."

## On negotiation

"Sometimes when a buyer is in town for just a week, and does not have all the information on comparable sales, then he may bargain harder. Sometimes a harder bargain is the result of unrealistic expectation on the part of the local seller. The buyer may well be presenting his best price, but doesn't want to pay what the seller is asking, then he will express his objections by way of a lower offer."

"If I feel his offer is not going to work, I will explain to him why it will not work, show him the comparables, and suggest some alternative approaches. At the end, it usually works out as long as both sides have good will."

## On cultural knowledge

"I was married to a Japanese woman who helped me understand the importance of face and mutual respect. I always insist that people go through a door before me, and I treat local people just the same."

"I think a lot of people get all caught up with *fēng shuǐ*. Replace the word '*fēng shuǐ*' with 'functional' and you will be able to take the mystery away from what is essentially a different interpretation of common sense."

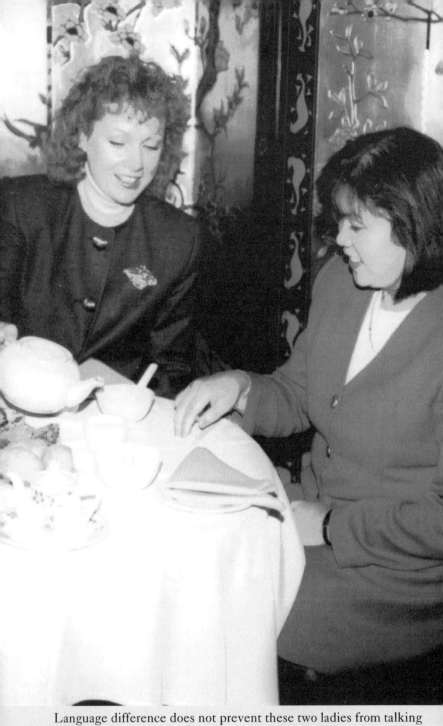

Language difference does not prevent these two ladies from talking business over *dim sum*. The lady (right) shows an appreciative hand gesture when she is served tea.

(Photo courtesy of Robert Cheng)

# Chapter Eleven

# $\mathscr{C}$ommunicating Across A Language Difference

One of the most difficult things front-line workers have to do is communicate with customers who have limited knowledge of English. The experience is frustrating, time-consuming and often results in unnecessary misunderstanding. This chapter will discuss:

- Learning a new language.
- Communicating through an interpreter.
- Communicating without an interpreter.
- Communicating over the telephone.
- Non-verbal communications.
- Learning Chinese.

## *Learning a new language*

Most Chinese customers can speak some English, but with differing degrees of fluency. Surveys show that only a small minority of the Chinese people in Canada have no knowledge of English at all.[1] However, being able to speak limited English does not mean one will feel comfortable using the language in a transaction. If you imagine you are travelling in a foreign country and must converse in an unfamiliar language, you can appreciate the problems involved.

Learning a second language is not easy. This is especially so when the new language has a linguistic structure very different from the mother tongue, such as a Chinese person trying to learn English as a second language. Most people take six to twelve months of total immersion to reach a level of proficiency sufficient to take care of everyday living. They will require five to seven years of immersion to be completely fluent. The period required to reach complete fluency also depends on age. About 45% of the Chinese people in Canada have been here for less than five years.[2] Many of them are still struggling to carry out their everyday activities in English.

Eventually, most people will reach a level of fluency which allows them to function well in the society. The difficult time is the transitional period. This is the time your customers need your understanding and support the most. If you can provide the required support with patience and understanding, you will not only win a customer but a friend.

## *Communicating through an interpreter*

You will be communicating through an interpreter if the customer has little or no knowledge of English, and the information you need from each other is too complex to be conveyed using simple words and hand signs. The interpreter may be someone in the customer's group, one of your fellow workers, or sometimes another customer. Here are some of the points to bear in mind when you are communicating with your customers through an interpreter:

- When the customer speaks, look at him even if you do not understand him, unless you notice that he is avoiding your eye contact.
- When the interpreter speaks, look at the interpreter and turn to the customer from time to time and acknowledge his points by nodding your head.
- When you speak, look at the customer instead of the interpreter even though he does not understand you.
- If you find out the customer can understand English after all, do not bring this to his attention. Continue with the interpretation process unless your customer decides to speak directly to you.
- Skillfully plant some questions in your message to see if you get the response you expect from your customers. Some interpreters, especially children, may not be able to relate your message accurately.
- Avoid colloquial or slang expressions. They seldom translate well.

## Communicating without an interpreter

You may not always have the luxury of an interpreter. In most cases, the customer will have a limited knowledge of English. If you see a lot of customers in this category, you may consider preparing some bilingual cue cards to cover the terms you use most often. Here are some do's and don'ts to remember when communicating with customers who are struggling with English:

*Do:*

- Be an exceptionally good listener.
- Speak slowly. What you consider as a normal speed is probably too fast for your customers.
- Use simple words and sentences.
- Refer to the actual object whenever appropriate. When referring to an object, use your open palm instead of an index finger. Some customers consider pointing as a rude gesture.
- Draw simple pictures to support your points.
- Summarize what you understand from the customer from time to time.

Don't:

- Use idiomatic expressions or slang.
- Raise your voice. Your customers do not have a hearing problem.
- Rely on body language.

### Communicating over the telephone

Talking over the telephone has two additional problems: First, you cannot see the customer's facial expressions and body gestures. Second, you may be passed around from one person to another and have to repeat explaining everything from scratch. There is very little you can do to avoid these problems, but there are things you can do to help you get your message across:

### General strategies

- All the points regarding communication without an interpreter still apply, except that you cannot draw pictures or refer to visible objects and bilingual language cards.

- Articulate more clearly than you normally do. For example, say "did you" instead of "did ja." Slow down your talking speed even further.
- Assess whether you can continue the conversation or you need to refer the call to someone who can speak Chinese.
- Do not pretend you understand if you do not.

## Incoming calls

It is very unlikely you will receive a call from someone who speaks no English at all. Customers who do not speak English usually ask someone who can to make the call on their behalf. Usually the problem lies in understanding someone who speaks only limited or heavily accented English. If the person speaks limited English, respond with simple sentences or even key words. If the person speaks fluent English but has a very strong accent, try to get him to slow down. In either case, paraphrase to let the customer know that you get his message.

To ask a customer to slow down without offending him, follow these strategies:

- Slow down yourself, and usually people will respond in kind.
- Say: "You are saying something very important. I want to be sure I understand it. Please slow down for me."

If nothing works and you decide to pass the call, say something like: "Can I ask Mr. Wong to call you back. He is an expert in this area and he speaks Cantonese. He can help you better than I can."

## Outgoing calls

When you call a Chinese household, you may be greeted with "hello" or with "*wèi*." A "hello" greeting usually means the person on the other end can speak English. A "*wèi*" greeting usually means the other person may or may not speak English. Incidentally, the Chinese word *wèi* has no specific meaning. It is just the way Chinese people answer the telephone. It signifies all of these meanings: "Hello, who is there? I am here, start speaking." The word is not used in everyday conversation.

Follow these strategies:

1. Make your calls after school or office hours. You will have a higher chance of speaking to someone who can speak English. (If you are calling a business, ignore this rule.)

2. Ask to speak to the person you want. From their response, you will know if the one who answers your call speaks English.

3. If the other person does not speak English, try to determine if he speaks Mandarin or Cantonese. A Mandarin-speaker answers a call with a "*wèi*" that sounds like the English word "way." A Cantonese-speaker answers with a "*wei*" that sounds like the English word "white" without the ending. In general, there are more customers in Canada who speak Cantonese than Mandarin.

4. Ask them in Cantonese or Mandarin whether anyone in the household can speak English by following

these clues. You may not be right but you should be close enough to get the message across. Try to practise with a Chinese friend first.

## Cantonese:

*"Yau mo yun gong ying mun?"* (Is there someone who can speak English?)

Expected responses:

| Response | Meaning |
| --- | --- |
| *Yau* | Yes, there is |
| *Mo* | No, there isn't |
| *Dun yud dun* | Please wait |

## Mandarin:

*"Yǒu rén jiǎng yīngyǔ ma?"* (Is there someone who can speak English?)

Expected responses:

| Response | Meaning |
| --- | --- |
| *Yǒu* | Yes, there is |
| *Méi yǒu* | No, there isn't |
| *Děng yī děng* | Please wait |

Obviously it is impossible to anticipate all possible responses. The suggested ones above are the more frequently used responses to the question.

5. If the other side still speaks to you in Chinese, say you will have someone to call them back at a later time.

Cantonese:

*"Chee dee dah farn bay lay."* (Will call you back later.)

Mandarin:

*"Dĕng yī huir gĕi nĭ huí diànhuà."* (Will call you back later.)

6. Call back at a later time, or have someone who can speak Chinese call for you.

## Non-verbal communication

We all communicate with body language, whether we are conscious of it or not. The problem is, people from different cultures have different body languages. Since body language is not something usually taught in school, even if a person is fluent in English, he can still misread your non-verbal signals. On the other hand, it will help you to understand your customers more if you can read their body language. This section describes what signals you should not use and what signals you can expect to see from your Chinese customers.

### Signals you should not use

These hand signals have no meaning at all to a Chinese customer unless he has been exposed to North American culture:

- The okay sign (making a circle with the thumb and the index finger).
- Crossing the fingers to symbolize good luck.
- The Hawaiian hand signal for "take it easy" (raising your thumb and pinky simultaneously).

## *Frequently observed signs from a Chinese customer*

To say "good" or "great," a Chinese customer will usually raise a thumb and push his closed fist forward forcefully by a few inches.

To say "there is none," the usual gesture is to stretch out both arms to the side with the palms opened facing the front.

To say "no," a Chinese customer will wave an opened hand in front of them a few times with the palm side facing out. Since Chinese people are not used to saying "no," you need to assess from the situation whether the customer is really rejecting your proposal, or whether he is behaving *kè qì* (guest behaviour). Here are some examples:

> You went out with your customer for a Chinese lunch called *Dim Sum*. This is the type of lunch in which dishes are brought to your table on push-carts. When a cart arrives, you make your selection on the spot by either asking for a dish or letting it pass. At one point, the waitress brought in a cart. The customer waved his hand to make a "no" signal. This was a simple "no" since no face was involved.

> During lunch you made a business proposal. The customer was interested and the two of you were exchanging details. Over a certain minor point the customer suddenly waved his hand a few times to express his objection. This was a "no" since the customer was in major agreement with you but differed in opinion over a trivial point. If it had been a major point, the customer would not likely say "no" so quickly, but express his reservation in some other ways.

> You remembered this customer had paid for your lunch

last you dined together and you felt it was your turn to return the favour. You offered to pay for him, but the customer objected by vigorously waving his right hand. This is probably a *kè qì* behaviour. Your best policy is to insist on paying in spite of his objections. On the other hand, if you had paid for his lunch a number of times, the "no" would probably be genuine since he felt he would lose face if he continued to allow you to pay.

### Gestures indicating objection or dissatisfaction

The above example indicated that although Chinese people say "no" by waving their hands, the gesture does not always mean they object. Since many Chinese people feel it is inappropriate to express an objection directly, objections are normally expressed in more subtle ways. Here are some of the common ones, representing different levels of objection or dissatisfaction:

- Making an almost inaudible "jig" sound by placing the tongue on the front end of the palate and pulling it back. This means "there is a little problem."
- Drawing in air between clenched teeth, making a "hissing" sound. This means "I am sensing a serious problem."
- Shrugging the shoulders. This means "oh, well."
- A forced smile. The customer is in effect saying "Anything you say."
- An unusually long pause without reply or acknowledgement. This means "I don't like what I'm hearing, but go on."
- Giving you a deliberate momentary glance. He is now telling you "I'm giving you a hint, please pick up my clue."
- Cold hard stare. This is a serious warning, meaning "You're beginning to talk as if you're not on my side."

## Learning Chinese

It is tremendously advantageous to learn the customers' language, even if you can only manage a limited number of words and simple expressions.

Your local school boards and a number of commercial language institutes offer Mandarin and Cantonese courses. The David Lam Centre at Simon Fraser University also has excellent Chinese language courses for the public. These courses have helped many business people to gain the necessary language skills to do business with Chinese people in Asia. Less involved than courses are audio tapes. Many of the commercially available tapes are meant for Westerners planning to travel into China.

You may also consider learning the language in some less formal ways. A good way is to learn it from your Chinese-speaking friends. Another way is to watch Chinese television channels, such as your local multicultural channel and Chinese television stations. Watching Chinese television programs gives you the additional advantage of watching the body language, expressions and way of life of your customers. Even if you do not understand the conversation or narration, you will still be able to pick up some isolated expressions.

## *Learning the Chinese Language and Culture*

Dr. Jan Walls is a professor at the David See-Chai Lam Centre for International Communication. I met Dr. Walls for the first time during a conference where a number of world-renowned scholars presented their thoughts on the challenges facing the Chinese culture today. I was thoroughly moved by his presentation, which was done in both Mandarin and English. I have met many Caucasians who have a mastery of the Mandarin language, but rarely have I come across someone who has as deep an understanding of the Chinese culture.

**Author:** Dr. Walls, you know a lot about the Chinese culture, more so than many of us ourselves. What prompted you to be interested in our culture?

**Dr. Walls:** It started with a need to understand myself and my own culture. I wanted to get an understanding of myself from another angle, one that is outside of my own culture.

**Author:** How long have you been studying Asian cultures?

**Dr. Walls:** 34 years.

**Author:** How long did it take you to become fluent in Mandarin?

**Dr. Walls:** About a year to acquire a modest vocabulary.

**Author:** What is the best way to learn the culture?

**Dr. Walls:** Watch Chinese movies. Learn about what constitutes acceptable behaviour, and people's expectations in different situations.

**Author:** As someone who has learned a great deal about Chinese language and culture, what would you consider were some of the initial challenges?

**Dr. Walls:** I found Mandarin an easy language to speak but somewhat difficult to read and write at the beginning. The bigger challenge however was not the language itself, but understanding the context in which something is said. In any language, there are always presuppositions behind what is spoken. This is true even for Anglo-Canadian culture, and is more so in Chinese culture.

**Author:** What would you suggest a non-Chinese person to do to overcome these differences in communication pattern?

**Dr. Walls:** You must "empty your mind" and focus on the situation to figure out the expectation.

**Author:** From your observation of the Chinese people, what are some of the things Chinese people would like others to understand?

**Dr. Walls:** That they are a well-educated and well-cultured people by world standards.

### *The Lighter Side of Language Difference*

A Caucasian friend of mine who was born and raised in China recently visited his birthplace. After doing a walking tour of the city, he was unable to find the way back to his hotel. Just at that time, he saw a couple of Chinese women coming his way. He asked the first woman in perfect Mandarin about the way to the hotel. The woman looked at him, shook her head, then went on her way. He then asked the second woman, who again looked at him, shook her head, and went on. A few seconds later, he heard the two women speaking to each other: "I'm sure he just asked us how to get to Xin Hua Hotel," one said. "But what could I tell him? I don't speak English!"

&ast; &ast; &ast;

A customer who speaks very limited English called to enquire if his payment had been received. After figuring out what his concern was and checking on the record, the secretary told him: "Sir, you paid. We got."

&ast; &ast; &ast;

It was during a dinner conversation that I first heard people say "It's a piece of cake." I was somewhat confused since everyone was eating chocolate pudding at the time.

&ast; &ast; &ast;

When President Clinton was visiting Russia, he made an "Okay" sign with his right hand to the crowd, not realizing that it was a very rude thing to do in Russia.

*  *  *

Here is a famous one from another U.S. president: During his visit to Berlin, President Kennedy announced before an enthusiastic crowd: "*Ich bin ein Berliner!*" Translated literally, it means "I am a Berliner." Yet the people in Berlin do not call themselves Berliners, and use the term to mean a type of doughnut!

---

[1] DJC Research. "Market Overview" in *The Chinese Consumer in Canada* 1995, p.14.

[2] Ibid., p.5.

Signs of interest are often easy to detect, regardless of the customer's cultural background.
(Photo courtesy of Robert Cheng)

# Chapter Twelve

# *G*enerating Interest
# and Handling Objections

To be able to generate interest in your customers and handle their objections is a critical skill in selling. To generate interest, you need to understand what motivates your customers and how to read their signs of interest. To handle objections, you need to know what turns your customers off, how to read warning signs and address concerns in a manner that befits their culture. Since Chinese customers are not always explicit about what they like or dislike, many non-Chinese salespeople find it difficult to understand their needs. This chapter will discuss:

- Value drivers
- Signs of interest
- Hidden concerns
- Handling objections
- Meeting the expectations of your customers

## *Value drivers*

To spark interest, you must find out what is important to your customer. Although the Chinese customers are driven by the same set of values as consumers of other cultures, there are differences in their relative importance. For the purpose of this chapter, I will use the term "value drivers" to describe factors that are important to the Chinese people when it comes to making a purchasing decision. Understanding these value drivers not only helps to identify which product groups the Chinese consumers buy, but their feature preferences and how one should position a product.

While specific value drivers differ from customer to customer, most Chinese customers found the following drivers important. The first three are supremely important and the rest are relatively important:

- Protecting the well-being of their families.
- Giving their children a good education.
- Making or saving money.
- Saving time and trouble.
- Enhancing their self-esteem.

***Well-being of their family members:*** This is an important concern for people of many cultures, and is supremely important for the Chinese people. A common Chinese well-wish is *lǎo shào píng ān*, meaning peace and health to the young and old. Concern about safety and health of family members is one of the underlying reasons many Chinese people select houses consistent with the *fēng shuǐ* principles, or cars made by certain manufacturers. This concern is so overbearing that most Chinese buyers will shy away from products with potential safety hazards whether these hazards are real or imaginary.

A realtor once told a story that illustrates the seriousness of this concern for Chinese buyers. One day he showed a home to a new immigrant from Hong Kong. The house backed onto a green belt which drew the attention of the customer more than a few times. After spending a long time in the house, the customer asked if there were coyotes in the area. The realtor replied: "You don't have to worry about coyotes. They were all eaten up by the bears." The customer disappeared in no time and the realtor never had a chance to explain it had all been meant as a harmless joke!

*Children's education:* Another value driver that is supremely important to the Chinese people is their children's education. The emphasis on education is ingrained into the Chinese cultural conscience. John Naisbitt even went as far as saying that giving their children a good education is a universal Chinese obsession.[1] This applies equally to formal school education and extracurricular activities, such as piano and art lessons. Many Chinese parents divert a great deal of resources into these areas. Some parents will relocate so that their children can attend what they perceive as a better school. This concern drives many Chinese parents to look for products or services that will help their youngsters do well in school or be more well-rounded achievers. Many privately run programs, such as after-school mathematics enhancement, computer, music and Chinese lessons have all benefited from this value driver.

*Money:* A third supreme value driver is money. It is fair to say that most Chinese people are hardworking and thrifty. This is especially true for the Overseas Chinese. As a people, they are more inclined to take risks and work longer hours in order to create wealth. If your product can potentially enhance their wealth, it will be looked at favourably. This is one of the reasons why investment securities and lotteries sell very well to the Chinese. As consumers, they are very concerned about costs. While no one, regardless of culture, feels good paying too much for an item, many Chinese consumers may feel guilty buying something they have no need to buy and feel foolish paying more than what they should pay. This does not mean Chinese buyers will always buy something cheap, but it means they will generally shop for what they need rather than want, and get the best perceived value for the dollars. It also means they will be interested in products that are durable and cost less to operate. For example, one of the features they may look for in buying an appliance is that it does not use too much electricity.

**Convenience and efficiency:** This is an understandable factor for people who came from a fast-lane type of culture. This means if you can provide a product or service that can save them time or trouble, you will get their interest. A good application of this is a good warranty or maintenance program that comes with the product. It also means if you are able to provide a product or service in less time and with less trouble than your competitors, you will have an edge.

**Self-esteem:** This is a value driver for many Chinese, but few would buy something purely based on self-esteem alone. For example, many Chinese people like to buy things with good brand names, partly due to esteem and partly due to the quality behind these brand name products. If the purchaser is satisfied with the requirements of quality and cost, self-esteem will be their next factor to consider.

These five value drivers are not the only ones pertinent to Chinese consumers, but are the most important ones. Recognizing these values will help you interpret the buying signals discussed in the next section.

## *Signs of interest*

Many Westerners say they find it difficult to read the buying signals from their Chinese customers. Often they had initial doubts whether a Chinese customer was serious because he showed almost no sign of interest, and then they were completely taken by surprise when the customer placed a handsome order at the end.

It is simply not true that Chinese consumers do not show their interest or preferences. Unless a customer has no intention of buying, he will always tell you what he needs and likes. However, due to different communication patterns and their concern for face and negotiation position, you may need to listen to more than simple verbal messages. It also helps to remember some of the value drivers to put your observations in the proper context.

The Chinese people use two different words for listening: *wén* and *tīng*. The word *wén* (聞) is composed of two symbols, a door and an ear. It implies hearing some information. The word *tīng* (聽) is composed of the following symbols: ear, king, ten, eye (written horizontally), one, heart. It implies listening to the speaker with the ears, the eyes and with one heart as if the speaker is a king. This is a much deeper level of listening than just hearing. It also implies that listening takes more than just the ears, as one needs to watch (eyes) and process the information (heart) at the same time.

The key to uncovering your customers' preferences is to listen and observe. Listen to the background information about themselves, such as how long they have been in the country, their family size, the ages of their children and seniors. Listen to the questions which reflect their concerns. Listen to messages both said and unsaid. Observe where in the showroom they spend more of their time or which items or features their eyes rest upon. Observe any subtle but sudden change of tone, facial expression, body gesture and pace of movement. These are important clues indicating either excitement or disappointment.

Although Chinese customers may not express their excitement as openly as most other customers, there are still a lot of signs you can read if you know what to look for. Many of these signs are not too different from people belonging to other cultures, only that they are often more subtle for the Chinese people. Here are some common ones:

- The customer will discuss with his group about his thoughts, usually in Chinese.
- They may pass the merchandise around or spend a longer time at a particular place.
- They may come back for another visit, bringing someone else (usually a friend who is an "expert") with them.
- They begin to talk about how the merchandise can be used (e.g. how to fit furniture into a house, or people into a car, etc.).
- They may ask a lot of questions about the merchandise.
- They may begin to scrutinize or even to mildly criticize the item.

- There may be a sudden change in their body gesture or pace of movement.

Once you detect some signs of interest, elaborate on the benefits you feel are important to the customer. Offer a small discount or some added values to encourage him. Some added values that can interest your Chinese customers include complimentary gifts, coupons for future purchases, free delivery for bulky items and complimentary maintenance service. You may try to close but do not rush or pressure your customer. Always be resourceful, understanding and helpful. Solve his problems as if they were your own. If your product meets your customers' needs and you are there as a friend to them, they will buy from you.

## Hidden concerns

What customers say or do may be complicated by hidden concerns, such as face and negotiation position. I say "may be" because not all Chinese people behave like this, and a growing number like the straight-forwardness of Western communication style. When a customer has hidden concerns, it is possible that he will act unnaturally. Here are some common ones:

*Obligation:* When a customer is not yet ready to buy but wants some information from you, he may have a hidden concern about obligation. This situation usually arises when a customer needs something but does not have enough knowledge about the product or price to make a purchasing decision. Typically, the customer will shop around and ask a number of questions. His dilemma at this point is, he needs your service but does not want to feel obliged to buy from you. For this reason, some customers

261

may ignore the approach of a salesperson, or may not tell the salesperson about true needs. When you feel that the customer is somewhat elusive about his needs, your best policy is to make a few recommendations, explain that your job is to help, take on a slightly passive role, observe the customer's interest, and be ready to provide any assistance. When the customer feels that you are sincere in helping him without obliging him to buy from you, he will usually open up to tell you his needs.

*Face:* If a customer is willing to pay only within a certain price range but is concerned that you may look down on his wealth position, he may have a hidden concern about saving face. Typically, a customer in this situation will either elude your question about how much he is prepared to pay, or will give you a price well above the true range he intends to pay. Your best response is to present him with examples of merchandise in different price ranges, and focus on the benefits of each one. Pinpoint something unique in each example. When you sense that your customer is paying more attention to a particular item, casually mention how other customers also like this item.

*Over-payment:* A customer will feel concerned when he sees suitable product at a price he is willing to pay but suspects that the item or its substitute may be available at a lower price somewhere else. Customers with this hidden concern may pretend that they are just browsing. They will, however, take note of features and price information for comparison. Some may purposely look for something in a lower price bracket just to see if they can find what they need without having to pay as much. If you sense that your customer is pleased with a product but hesitates to make a commitment, or if he pays keen attention to prices and features but does not verbally express interest, he may be concerned about overpayment. To address his concern, highlight the unique benefits of the product you are selling, encourage him to shop around and if appropriate, offer him in writing to match any lower price he can find within a certain period after the purchase.

*Negotiating position:* When a customer is interested in a certain item, he may have a concern about jeopardizing his negotiating position if he reveals too much interest. If you notice your customer pays a lot of attention to an item and at the same time expresses some negative comments, take that as a good clue. To openly criticize something or someone is not natural to the Chinese cultural behaviour. In many cases they are doing it to set the stage for negotiation. If the customer is criticizing an item, acknowledge his comments and ask how much the item is worth to him despite the shortcoming. Be careful, however, to differentiate between fake criticism and genuine concern about possible shortcomings with the product. Fake criticism is usually directed at things that cannot be corrected or substituted. Genuine concern is usually associated with a real problem that could be corrected.

*Belief:* Some customers may have a hidden concern about numbers, directions, dates, or colours but do not want you to think that they are superstitious. Typically, they will ask whether there is any other choice of, say, numbers available. Your best strategy is to learn about the common taboos in your industry, and provide customers with a mix of choices with at least one or two good selections. Alternatively, you may like to ask what, for example, date of delivery they have in mind. If your customer is apologetic about choosing a very unusual date, assure him that a lot of people do the same. You might add that, in fact, he is doing you a favour by allowing you to spread the orders throughout the month.

## *Handling objections*

If Westerners have a hard time reading signs of interest in Chinese customers, they will have an even harder time reading their signs of objections. The thousands of years of cultural conditioning and concern over harmony have trained most Chinese people to restrain outright objections and oppositions. In many cases, they can only be felt but not heard. To those inside the culture, such subtle objections are as loud as a cannon. To those not familiar with the culture, they may miss out some very important clues. There are seven major reasons why a customer, Chinese or not, objects to buying a product or service:

- The product does not meet the customer's needs or requirements.
- The product costs more than the perceived benefits.
- The customer does not have enough money or credit to pay for it.
- The product does not appeal to the customer's personal likes and dislikes.
- The logistics, such as delivery schedule or assembling procedures, do not suit the customer.
- The customer's lack or misunderstanding of product knowledge.

- Some product features or characteristics are contrary to the customer's beliefs or preferences.

A customer may show his objections in a number of ways. In many cases, he will tell you directly, either verbally or using non-verbal signs such as drawing air between clenched teeth. Alternatively, he may suddenly change the topic of discussion, drag his feet or come up with some flimsy excuses. If your customer is forthright in telling you his objection, your battle is half-won. It is always a lot easier to overcome objections when you know what they are.

The problem comes when your customer is not vocal about his objections. You may sense it, but you can never be sure why he objects. You may need to do some guess work. When you begin to sense objection from your customer, think back to the last thing you said. Put yourself in his shoes and try to assess the reasons behind the objection, whether it be financial, logistical, or otherwise. Respond by providing your customer with a few alternatives. Observe your customer's reaction to those alternatives, and you can then fine tune your suggestions until you find one that your customer likes.

If you feel a great deal of reluctance from your customer, do not press for a settlement. Suggest your customer to take some time to consider your offer. This "time-out" period can serve two purposes: (1) it allows both sides to reconsider their positions; (2) it relieves the customer of the burden of having to say "no" to you. Call him the next day or so to say you would really like to do business with him and ask him what you can do to make this happen. At this point, he may tell you his position or continue to show reluctance. Re-examine your offer to see if there is anything else you can do to reduce your customer's reluctance. If you have done everything you can and the customer still objects, your product probably does not meet his requirements in price or quality.

If there is a time-limit during the "time-out" period, tell the customer what the limit is and the reason behind it and offer your sincere help in answering any questions he may have in the meantime. Do not artificially create a reason just to put pressure on him. This sort of tactic usually back-fires. Call him shortly before the deadline to see if he needs any help or additional information. Ask him to call you if he accepts your offer or needs further assistance. Tell him if he does not call you back, you will understand and would like to be given another opportunity to serve him again in the future.

If you sense that your customer is using an excuse to turn your offer down, treat the excuse as if it is a true reason. That way, you will not inadvertently trivialize a true concern, nor will you unintentionally cause your customer to lose face. Tell the customer that it is unfortunate, but you do understand. Do not say the decision is "disappointing" as some customers may feel they have upset the harmony between the two of you, and may avoid you in the future. In so doing, you will take the burden of having to say a flat "no" off your customer's shoulder, and have maintained face for both sides.

## Expectations of your customers

There are four things most Chinese customers expect of their salespeople:

*Good product knowledge:* This is important at all phases of the sale. Being new to the country, many Chinese customers rely on you to give them the needed information to make a purchasing decision. If they feel that you do not even know the product you are selling, they will look for someone else who can give them more confidence.

*Efficiency:* For customers who are used to an environment where efficiency is the only way of life, they can quickly become impatient with inefficient salespeople or inefficient systems. Once they find another vendor who is more efficient, they will not hesitate to make the move. Efficiency, however, does not mean rush. It means make things simple and readily available.

*Personal care:* Chinese people may treat a salesperson as "a stranger" or as "an associate," depending on how much personal care the salesperson provides. If you show you are there because your firm pays you to be there, they will react to you no differently from the way they would react to a stranger. Their relationship with you will be limited only to that particular transaction. They do not feel a need to be loyal to you, and do not expect you to provide anything more than the particular transaction requires. On the other hand, if you care for them the way a friend would, and find solutions to their problems and needs, they will regard you as an associate. They will seek you out the next time they enter your office or store, and will generally be loyal to you as long as you keep up your level of service.

As their associate, they do expect you to provide them a personal service. At the very least you will remember their names and family needs. They will expect you to be up front with them about the benefits and shortcomings of your product, and to advise them not only as a salesperson but as a friend.

It is possible that some of your customers may ask you to do small favours outside of the scope of your work. Many Western salespeople have difficulties with this because their business culture clearly separates work from personal favours. Here is an interesting paradox: most salespeople probably would not think twice about buying their customers something like a box of chocolate after the customers buy a large item, such as a house, from them. How is it that some salespeople would feel uncomfortable about running a small errand for a customer who hardly knows the city? To most newcomers, the greatest gift is your help, not a box of chocolate.

Many Chinese realtors, for example, volunteer their service to do a myriad of things for their newcomer customers, from receiving them into their homes to arranging telephone services for them. One car salesman went to the customer's home to change a flat tire for him one evening two weeks after he sold him the car. Through such favours they develop their bonds and become the customer's true friends. Friends usually buy from friends and refer other friends to them.

To what extent you wish to accommodate your customers' needs outside of your scope of work is your decision. Here are some guidelines for your consideration:

- Never agree to do anything illegal or immoral. In the overwhelming majority of the cases, your customers will not request these sort of favours. But if they do, you ought to decline.
- Never do anything you feel reluctant to do.
- Always do a favour because you wish to help, not to oblige.
- Accept that your customer may not buy from you in spite of your favours. Doing favours is like making an investment. You must do it wisely, but do not expect you will always win.

*Flexibility.* One requirement that makes your customers look at you as their "own friend" is your flexibility. We all know that every firm has its rules and policies. These rules and policies are supposed to help the firm do business more effectively. At the same time, customers are humans, not products that come off an assembly line. Each customer has individual needs and circumstances. When a rule becomes a hindrance to meeting the customer's needs, the rule itself may need to be re-examined. Many Chinese customers expect a salesperson to have the flexibility to challenge an outdated and unproductive rule, and come up with a creative but legal solution in order to meet their needs.

## Legendary Services

*Case 1*

During a meeting of a professional organization, a Caucasian lady once told the audience about a recent experience of legendary service she encountered in Japan.

One early afternoon when she and her companion were riding a taxi in Tokyo, she noticed the cab was a Honda similar to the model she drove at home, and the driver's seat had an attractive seat cover she had not seen before. On learning that the cover was made by Honda, she asked the driver to take them to a Honda service outlet.

It was not easy to explain to the salesman about her need, but the salesman was polite and patient. Through diagrams, broken English and broken Japanese, the salesman finally understood what she wanted. He apologized that in Japan their seat sizes are smaller and they did not make the covers suitable for the American-size seats. Then he added that he should be able to arrange a special one made for her, to be delivered to her hotel by 10 p.m.

The lady did not really think the salesman was serious. After spending the afternoon in the nearby neighbourhood, they were back to the hotel at about 9 p.m. Less than an hour later, there was a knock at the door. Outside was a messenger boy holding a silver plate. On top of the plate was a package and a letter, which said:

*Dear Ms. Brown:*

*We apologize for not having the seat cover you needed when you visited us this afternoon. We have arranged to have one made to fit the size of your car. In consideration of your inconvenience, we would like to present you this silver plate as a token of thanks for doing business with us in spite of our shortcomings. Please accept our sincere apology.*

*Signed, Vice-President of Sales*

Not everyone in sales is able to make the sort of generous decision the vice-president in the above story could make. Here is something that happened to me more than 20 years ago and I still remember it today. It shows how a very ordinary transaction can still be extraordinary to a customer when the salesperson is friendly, caring and flexible.

## Case 2:

One day during my first year in Canada, I walked into a Toronto shoe store with an acute pain on one of my toes on the left foot. The shoes I had been wearing never fit me very well and the long walk that day had taken its toll. I was almost limping when I entered the store.

"Looks like you need a new pair of shoes," said the saleslady. "Let me offer you my assistance."

After listening to the problems I had with my own shoes, she explained the pain was partly caused by a misfit and partly by insufficient cushioning and air circulation. She then showed me how her shoes were constructed to provide the cushioning and

271

circulation I needed, and asked me to try out a pair.

When I put on the shoes, I was not entirely satisfied. While I was searching for the right word from my then limited English vocabulary, she said: "It seems these may be just a touch too small for you. Let me get you a larger pair."

She went into the backroom and reappeared with a new pair in less than a minute. In the meantime, I noticed that I only had trouble with the left shoe. The right shoe fit very well.

"Here, try this pair. It's half a size larger." I tried the new pair. This time my left shoe fit perfectly but the right was a touch too large. It kept slipping off. I explained my problem.

"Oh, it's a very common problem," she said. "Our two feet are not always the same size. About 10 to 15% of my customers have similar problems. You just have one foot slightly larger than the other."

I really liked the shoes, but did not want to have a pair that either hurt my left foot or kept slipping off my right. The saleslady must have read the doubt on my face. She picked up one shoe from each pair and said: "Here, try them in this combination."

No doubt the shoes fit this time, since they were two different sizes.

"But what would you do with the remaining shoes?" I asked.

"Not to worry," she said. "I have just as many customers who have the reverse problem. You take care of yourself first."

I walked out of the store with a "pair" of comfortable shoes and the recognition that this saleslady tried to solve the problem for me instead of just trying to sell me a pair of shoes. In the process, she impressed me with her product knowledge, her efficiency, her flexibility and her ability to read and respond to a customer's concerns. For a young fellow far from home, she acted more as a friend than a salesperson.

For all of that, I call the service she provided that day a legendary service.

---

[1] Naisbitt, John. *Megatrends Asia*. New York: Simon & Schuster, 1996. p.30

Taking part in a common activity is a good way to network.  People of many cultural origins participate in the annual Walk With the Dragon, a major fundraising activity for S.U.C.C.E.S.S.
(Photo courtesy of S.U.C.C.E.S.S.)

# Chapter Thirteen

# *N*etworking with Your Customers

> If we count the economic activity of all the Overseas Chinese as a country all by itself, it would be outranked only by the United States and Japan...The family businesses of the Overseas Chinese...constitute a huge global Chinese network of networks.
>
> John Naisbitt in *Megatrends Asia*

It is always advantageous to network in any business. It is especially advantageous to network with people who already have existing networks. In so doing you connect yourself to a web of resources, both local and international, as well as vastly broadening your potential customer base. Networking with your Chinese customers is like getting a gateway to the Internet. It is inexpensive and the potential return sees no bounds. What is more, you do not have to travel to Asia to be connected to this network.

Chinese people welcome those of other cultures into their networks. They realize that nothing can function and flourish in isolation, least of all business. The Chinese concept of open friendship can be summarized by the old aphorism: "Within the four seas, all of us are siblings."

Networking means relationship building. In Chinese society, there are three types of relationships between people. The first is an affective relationship, in which resources are shared and members of the network are related by blood, marriage, or long term friendship. The second is an instrumental relationship, in which resources are traded and members of the network are related strictly by a customer-supplier relationship. The third type is a hybrid of the first two, in which resources are partly shared and partly traded. Although not impossible, it is unlikely that you will develop the first type of relationship with your customers. The first 12 chapters of this book show you how to develop the second type of relationship with Chinese people. This chapter discusses how to develop the third type, also known as *guān xì*, or connection. Specifically, this chapter deals with these topics:

- Where can you start?
- Chinese social etiquette
- Building trust
- Using an intermediary
- Conflict resolution

## Where can you start?

The best place to start networking is with your own customer base. Your customers will tell their friends, relatives and neighbours about your products and services. What they say depends on their past experience with you. In the final analysis, how much new business your existing customers bring to you depends on the way you have treated them in previous transactions, the quality of your product and your integrity.

Other places to start building your network include trade associations, social clubs, community organizations, parent groups, churches, community school classes and so on. Depending on the nature of your business, certain organizations are more suitable than others for your networking purposes.

For example, trade associations are excellent means to network with firms that have similar business goals and problems. There are a number of Chinese trade associations in all major cities in the country. Though predominantly Chinese, they all welcome firms and individuals from other cultures. By joining these associations, not only will you be able to network with other members of the association, you can also get first hand experience of Chinese business life.

Another way to start your network is to take part in some leisure activities a lot of Chinese people enjoy. For example, you may consider joining a recreation or country club with a high number of Chinese members. Many Chinese people like to play golf, tennis, ping-pong and pool. They also enjoy bowling, skiing, *Tai Chi*, other forms of martial arts, *Mah Jong*, betting on horses, Karaoke singing and fishing.

## Chinese social etiquette

### General greetings

Most Chinese in North America will greet you with standard Western greetings. As a relationship develops, formal greetings will often be replaced with less formal ones. Here are some examples of less formal greetings Chinese people use.

Mandarin

| | |
|---|---|
| *Zĕn me yàng?* | (How's it going?) |
| *Chí le méi yŏu?* | (Have you eaten yet?) |
| *Qù năr?* | (Where are you heading?) |

Cantonese

| | |
|---|---|
| *Dim ah?* | (How's it going?) |
| *Sig jaw farn may ah?* | (Have you eaten yet?) |
| *Hui bean ah?* | (Where are you heading?) |

You will note that two greetings — "Have you eaten yet?" and "Where are you heading?" — are really not greetings in English. They are roughly equivalent to a greeting such as "What's happening?" in the North American culture. They are meant to be a greeting signal more than an enquiry.

You will certainly be able to build closer relationships with your Chinese associates if you learn to say these greetings in Chinese. Do not, however, use them the first time you meet a person, just as in English people usually do not say "How's it going?" unless you already know the person.

If you do not feel comfortable saying the greetings in Chinese, simply greet your customers the way you normally would in English. Do not greet with an English translation of the Chinese greeting. For example, if you say "Have you eaten yet?" or "Where are you heading?" in English, your Chinese associates are likely going to interpret your questions literally within the English context. On the other hand, it is quite possible that a Chinese new-comer may literally translate expressions such as "Have you eaten yet?" when he greets you. If your new Chinese friend one day comes to you with a rather unusual question, you will know why.

## Expressions of humility

When two people become more acquainted with each other, some of the earlier forms of *kè qì* behaviour will progressively decrease. This is a sign that the two people are drawing closer. Nevertheless, no matter how close they get, they always take extreme care not to upstage one another. This is critically important in building relationships with your Chinese associates.

Due to this cultural taboo, many Chinese people feel uncomfortable talking about their own accomplishments or receiving praise with a simple "thank you." This does not mean they do not like others to recognize their achievements. With exposure to Western cultures, more and more Chinese are now able to talk about their own accomplishments or accept praise. Yet the fundamental habit of self-deprecating is still distinctly noticeable. When socializing with Chinese associates, be prepared to hear a person belittling himself, or even his family. Your best response is to say the contrary. Here are two examples:

## Example 1:

| Associate: | I am really no good at this. It runs in the family. |
| You should say: | I think you are just too modest. I am sure you can do a good job. |
| Associate: | No, no. I'm really no good at it. |

| You should say: | If you are no good, then what about the rest of us? I guess some people are just not content with an A. |

**Example 2:**

| Associate: | Oh, that venture. I just broke even. |
| You should say: | You mean you broke the bank. |
| Associate: | No, no, I wish. I made at the most two pennies of profit. |
| You should say: | It sounds like two bundles of profit. |

This type of apparently meaningless exchange of self-deprecating and counteracting responses takes place between close associates many times a day. The key is to tirelessly recognize the other's achievements while downplaying one's own.

Be cognizant of the new generation of Chinese business people, many of them from Hong Kong. This group received Western education, but operated in a predominantly Chinese environment. Their exposure to both cultures has made them masters in both self-promotion and self-effacement.

There is no need to speak self-deprecatingly if it makes you feel uncomfortable. You can talk about your own accomplishments, but you should not brag. Bragging is poor taste in any culture. There is a general saying among the Chinese people: "A good flower does not have to tell people about its fragrance."

**Privacy**

Occasionally, some Chinese associates may ask questions that seem rather intrusive, such as your age, your wage, how much you paid for your house, its square footage and so on. By Western standards, these questions are clearly an intrusion of privacy, and deserve a rude response such as "none of your business." As more Chinese people are exposed to Western culture, more are beginning to respect others' privacy and will not ask this sort of questions. However, some are still unaware that this type of question is taboo in the West.

Privacy is not a Chinese concept. In fact there is no suitable translation for this term in Chinese. The closest equivalent in modern Chinese literature is *yǐn sī* (隱私), but this term literally means "hidden secrets" and carries a connotation that one is hiding something shameful from other people. In traditional Chinese society, much of what the West regards as "private information" is as private as the house number on your door. In fact, the two most often asked questions between new acquaintances in a very traditional social intercourse are:

> *Guì xìng?* (What is your honourable family name?)
> *Guì gēng?* (What is your honourable zodiac sign?)

The intent of the second question is to establish seniority between the two acquaintances. Age has never had any negative connotations in traditional Chinese thinking. It has always been associated with wisdom and honour, and is hardly regarded as private information.

Do not ask your Chinese associates any questions you normally would not ask any other colleagues in the Western context. On the other hand, if a new acquaintance asks you a nosy question, do not be annoyed or give him a lecture on privacy. If you feel comfortable sharing the information, simply answer the questions matter-of-factly. Otherwise, try to dodge it with a joke or a counter-question. Here is an example:

| | |
|---|---|
| Acquaintance: | How old are you? |
| You: | You want to take a guess? |
| Acquaintance: | You are so healthy looking it's hard to guess. What about forty? |
| You: | Ha, ha ... getting there, getting there. |

Then switch the topic.

## Chinese meals

Chinese people love going out to restaurants where a lot of networking and business deals are done. Eating is such an integral part of the Chinese culture it has been developed into an art. Sharing a good meal together is both a form of entertainment and a means of improving the relationship between you and your associates. It pays, therefore, to know something about the culinary aspects of Chinese culture.

Ask a Chinese friend to show you to some popular Chinese restaurants in your neighbourhood. Distinguish a traditional Chinese restaurant from one targeted to the North American public. A traditional Chinese restaurant usually serves *Dim Sum* for lunch and Chinese banquets for dinner. A North American Chinese restaurant serves chop suey, eggrolls and fortune cookies, all of which are ingenious inventions of the early Chinese immigrants to this continent, but are not traditional Chinese cuisine. If in doubt, look at the patrons to see whether a restaurant is traditional or North American. Most Chinese people go to traditional

Chinese restaurants.

*Dim Sum* is a special type of Chinese lunch that is very popular. Typically small dishes of delightful looking and tasting food are wheeled out of the kitchen on carts. When a cart arrives at your table, you can either ignore it or ask to have whatever dishes you wish. Once a dish is chosen, it is meant for everyone at the table rather than one particular person. The advantage of Chinese style eating is everyone can get a taste of every variety on the table. A good *Dim Sum* restaurant can easily carry 30 to 50 varieties. Some of the more popular ones among both Chinese and Caucasian customers are shrimp dumplings, sticky rice, rice rolls and egg tarts.

A Chinese banquet is truly an experience. Usually there are 10 to 12 courses from appetizers to desserts. Dishes are brought to the table one at a time, so remember: Don't keep eating one dish just because it is tasty, or else you may not have room for the rest.

Chinese tea is almost always served at Chinese meals. There are many varieties of Chinese tea, all of them are the green variety. Two common varieties include *xiāng piàn* (Jasmine tea) and *pú ěr* (oolong tea). If you do not like drinking plain green tea, order a soft drink or ask for a glass of water. You will notice that when tea is served to a Chinese associate, he will tap the table lightly with his index and middle fingers. This is a common gesture of thanks, only used when tea is served. You may imitate the gesture to demonstrate your knowledge of the culture, or you can simply say "thank you" the way you normally do.

Chinese people eat with chopsticks, and many North American friends have also learned to use them. Eating with chopsticks shows your respect for your associates' culture and helps to narrow the cultural gap in between. It is really not difficult. If you do not already know how to use them, ask a Chinese friend to teach you. It should take about five to ten minutes to learn the basic movements so that you will not starve, and about two or three meals of practice to become a master. There is no reason to be embarrassed if you have not mastered the basic movements. Your Chinese friends will understand.

In a typical Chinese table setting, you will find a small bowl and one or two small plates in front of you. Transfer your food from the serving dishes to the small bowl or one of the plates. If you have two plates in front of you, use one for bones and food scraps. Otherwise use the only plate for that purpose. In most restaurants the staff will replace your plate frequently enough that you will always have a clean one to use. You do not need a knife, because the food is already cut into bite-size pieces before it is served. If you come across a piece too large to put into your mouth, it is perfectly acceptable to bite off a part.

Be aware that many of the food pieces may come with bones. Again it is perfectly all right to bite off the meat from the bones. Some Chinese people may put the piece into the mouth, work at it and spit out the bones. You may not want to do the same because the practice is contrary to everything your mother taught you about table manners. The most graceful way to take care of the bones is to separate the meat from the bones in the bowl before you put it into your mouth. If your chopstick skill is not advanced enough for this rather complicated manoeuvre, put the piece into your mouth, work at it and then pull out the bones one at a time with your chopsticks.

Taking care of bones is not the only problem facing a person used to the very strict code of Western table manners. You may find some of your Chinese friends breaking every table rule imaginable. At times you may even find some of their eating behaviours unpleasant. Here is a partial list of what you may see:

- Eating with the body bent forward so that the mouth is only inches away from the bowl or plate.
- Looking at the food instead of at you.
- Chewing with the mouth open.
- Slurping.
- Bringing the bowl to the lips to shove food (usually rice) into the mouth.
- Speaking with food in the mouth.
- Biting a piece off with the incisors.
- Spitting bones out of the mouth.
- Using a toothpick to clean the teeth.

It is important to refrain from judging Chinese table manners by Western standards. Some of these behaviours, such as slurping, are also considered rude according to the very relaxed Chinese table rules. Your job is to build a relationship with Chinese acquaintances, not to educate them about etiquette. If their dining behaviour bothers you, look beyond it and concentrate on the conversation or the food. There is no need to follow their habits. Chinese table rules are so relaxed that you can still enjoy a Chinese meal without breaking any of your own rules. For example, if you do not feel comfortable bringing the bowl to your lips and shovelling rice into your mouth, use your chopsticks to bring rice to your mouth one heap at a time. This is somewhat inefficient but certainly looks more graceful by Western standards. In fact, more and more Chinese people are now eating rice in this manner, probably due to Western influence. And if all else fails, there is no reason why you cannot ask for a fork.

Some people are concerned about the hygiene of sharing a dish. Since all food pieces are cut bite-size and are selected individually, the chance of picking up germs from other people's chopsticks is small. In addition, most tables are set with serving spoons or tongs. If there is none on the table, you can always ask for one. Alternatively, many people invert their chopsticks and use the blunt ends to transfer food from the shared dishes to their individual bowl while using the pointed ends from bowl to mouth. If you are still concerned about catching germs, here is a trick. When a dish comes, you immediately stand up to serve everyone at the table. That way, you are guaranteed of getting an uncontaminated portion and you will also gain appreciation around the table for your masterful *kè qì* behaviour.

Some Westerners, especially those less adventurous diners, cannot bring themselves to try some of the more sophisticated Chinese ingredients, including chicken feet, jelly fish, bird's nest, snake meat, shark's fin and sea cucumber. Although the thought of eating these creatures may be revolting to some readers, they are actually delicacies for Chinese people. Many Westerners who try them have come to like them. Bird's nest soup, for example, is made of a very nutritious form of protein secreted only by

286

certain swallows. These protein secretions are carefully graded. The better grade nests are worth hundreds of dollars an ounce. Most people do not have a problem eating uncooked honey, which is a secretion from bees, but they have a problem eating a cooked secretion from birds. You are well advised to try these delicacies, but if you really have an uneasy feeling about them, do not force yourself. You will not offend anyone if you cannot eat certain types of food. We all have our personal dietary limitations. Many Chinese people, for example, cannot eat cheese. However, you should not make anyone feel that eating such food is barbarous. Here are some guidelines for Chinese table manners:

### *Do*

- Wait for the elder members of your group to be seated before sitting down.

- Serve tea to people near you.

- When a new dish arrives, serve others before yourself.

- When picking food from a communal dish, pick the pieces closest to you.

- Wait for the host to make the first move before eating.

### *Don't*

- Move a piece of food away with your chopsticks in order to reach the piece you desire. What your chopsticks touch is what you should pick up.

- Insert your chopsticks into the rice bowl and leave

them free standing.

- Poke into a piece of food with your chopsticks the way you would with a fork.

Do not be embarrassed if a piece of food slips out of your hold in mid-transfer. It happens sometimes even to Chinese people. When a piece falls onto the table, you may either ignore it or pick it up with your chopsticks and leave it along with the food scraps. Once a piece touches the table, it is generally not eaten.

The most important rule in eating a Chinese meal is to relax and be yourself. Most people are so busy eating they will not notice any small aberration of table manners. If you are overly conscious about what you can and cannot do at the table, your uneasy feeling will become a source of concern for others. Small offences of table rules are unimportant to most Chinese people. Whether you enjoy your meal and your host's hospitality is the important thing.

If no previous arrangement has been made about who is paying the bill, you may find yourself in the midst of a small battle when it comes time to leave. As a rule, unless arranged beforehand, Chinese people do not split the bill. The *kè qì* behaviour will kick in at this time and everyone will be fighting to pay for the meal. Sometimes the fighting can get rather vigorous, especially to people not accustomed to such scenarios. When the dust settles, generally the one who was on the receiving end the last time will end up paying. If neither one paid before, you will have to decide whether you want to owe or own the favour this time. If there is a host, there is no need to fight over the bill. To do so is to upstage the host and cause him to lose face. Thank your host enthusiastically before you depart and tell him how much you enjoyed the meal.

## Gift giving

Gifts are used frequently in relationship building among the Chinese. Here are some examples of occasions when one gives gifts:

- Visiting someone's home, especially for the first time or when invited to a meal.
- When invited to a banquet to celebrate someone's birthday, birth of a child or wedding.
- As a token of appreciation for a favour.
- Shortly before or during festivals, such as Chinese New Year, Mid-Autumn Festival and Dragon Boat Festival.

Some common gifts include fruit, wine, handicrafts, festive items such as moon cakes for Mid-Autumn Festival, or speciality items from your travels, such as macadamia nuts from Hawaii. Some more exotic gifts, if you think you need to spend the money, include original Chinese paintings, ginseng, and certain delicacies such as bird's nest. If you are not familiar with these items, you can always choose something such as crystals, silver plates, aged wine, or anything you normally give.

Never give a clock (watches are acceptable). The term "giving a clock" sounds the same as attending one's funeral in Chinese. You can understand why your customers may not be very pleased with that idea. Try not to give cut flowers unless you are giving roses to someone with whom you are romantically involved.

This is especially so for white flowers as they are generally used only in funerals and cemeteries. Avoid cut white chrysanthemums whether live or artificial. It is customary for Chinese women to wear a small white chrysanthemum on the head during a period of mourning. Potted flowers, however, do not have the same implication.

When you present your gift to a Chinese associate, do not be surprised if the recipient refuses it. If the refusal is both vocal and supported by waving the hands vigorously, you can almost be sure that it is just part of the *kè qì* behaviour. You should insist on presenting the gift in spite of the apparent objection. This will show you are both sincere and determined to give. If the recipient is serious in rejecting your gift, which is extremely rare because it will mean breaking relationship with you, he will reject it firmly, calmly and solemnly.

According to traditional Chinese culture, it is impolite to open a gift in front of the giver, unless so requested. In most cases, after unsuccessfully rejecting your gift, the recipient will give in and leave the gift to one side without opening it. Do not be worried, it will be opened. Foodstuffs such as fruits and candies may be opened immediately to be shared between the host and guests.

As immigrants make the adjustment to mainstream society, some of these gift-giving and gift-receiving behaviours are dropped. In their place are more Western behaviours, where one will accept the gift with a "thank you", open it and show you their surprise and delight at your thoughtful gesture.

## Building trust

Building trust is the ultimate purpose of networking. Although your Chinese associates may start some sort of business relationship with you shortly after meeting you, they will rarely venture into anything serious until you have earned their trust. Earning trust takes a very long time. As the Chinese people say: "It takes a long journey to know a horse's strength, and a long time to know a human's heart."

Trusting a person means you can rely on him to take care of certain things for you. It means you will not let him down, cheat on him or betray him. It means he can turn his back on you without having to worry. In North America, this level of trust is not always a prerequisite for doing business. There are business laws, contracts and the judicial system to guard against most forms of ill will or negligence. In Hong Kong, commercial laws are as comprehensive as in North America. However, due to a general reluctance to go to court and difficulty understanding legal technicalities, most business people in Hong Kong rely on personal trust as well as a detailed commercial contract before entering into a serious business relationship. In Taiwan, most business relationships are based on trust, augmented by an official contract. In mainland China, a business contract is only the physical representation of the trust between the concerned parties. Depending on where your associate comes from, he may have a different opinion of the value of a contract. And regardless of where he comes from, the element of trust is paramount.

Where there is trust, there is always the risk of betrayal. You may worry about your associates betraying you. They in turn may worry about you betraying them. One way to increase your associates' trust level in you is to increase your own risk level. This is in effect saying: "I am making myself more vulnerable because I trust that you will not take advantage of my weaker position. Please do the same thing for me." In a society that values reciprocity, this is a good strategy for encouraging your associates to take a risk with you so that you can prove your integrity.

Most Chinese people take a holistic approach in evaluating the trustworthiness of an associate. Unlike the Western concept of division of personal and business lives, many Chinese people look at the two aspects of a person together. They do not separate the John Doe who runs the shop from the John Doe who goes fishing with them. They will observe the minor details of a person over a long period of time to arrive at a conclusion about his character and integrity. There is a Chinese saying: "When observing a person, look at the small details." They know if you can lie to your neighbours after work, you can also lie to them at work. They will listen to your stories, achievements, worries, and problems. They will also watch your expressions, your eyes, your body gestures and your postures. They will take note of what you promised and what you delivered, however trivial. They will ask others who have had dealings with you before. They believe that a person may be able to fool some people with words over a short period of time, but he cannot fool a lot of people with deeds over a long period of time. In the end, they will also rely on their intuition, which often is a much more reliable tool than many people believe.

The only way to get your associates' trust is to earn it. The only way to earn it is to be trustworthy yourself. There is no substitute or shortcut. You make an agreement and you keep the agreement, every time, all the time.

## Using an intermediary

Sometimes an opportunity arises and you want to involve a Chinese business partner who may have the resources you need, but has not yet established a trusting relationship with you. These are the times you need an intermediary, someone who knows you and the intended business partner equally well. The intended partner may be willing to start a business venture with you on account of his trust of the intermediary. Identify the unofficial "people brokers" in your community. They are a very valuable resource. Do not let them down. If you turn out to be less than trustworthy, you destroy any trust you have built up, and on top of that you will also cause the intermediary to lose face. It is unlikely he will give you another chance.

## Conflict resolution

How you handle yourself in a conflict situation is the ultimate test of trust. One is often torn between two different goals: to resolve the immediate issue of conflict to one's favour, and to maintain the long-term relationship with the other party. Sometimes there is no congruence between these two goals, and one must choose between immediate or long-term concerns. Yet far too often the incongruity is unnecessary. In many cases, not only is it possible to meet both short-term and long-terms goals in resolving a conflict, but the conflict can be used to enhance your bond with the other party.

Very often conflicting parties fail to understand each other's concerns. Typically when a person receives complaint, he immediately puts himself in a defensive mode. Once entrenched in this mode, he will be busy protecting his own interests rather than resolving the problem jointly. A battle follows and the winner is the one who loses the least. This pattern often is repeated between two parties, whether or not they belong to the same culture. When the parties belong to different cultures, misunderstandings and misgivings can be greatly compounded.

The first step in resolving a conflict is to listen to the other party's concerns. At the very least, you should patiently wait until the other party finishes his complaints before you respond. This sounds like a simple thing to do but it involves overcoming three important hurdles.

The first hurdle is your own emotion. Conflict is never pleasant and complaints are never music to the ears. It is natural for one to react emotionally to a negative comment. However, unless one controls his own emotions at this stage, nothing the associate or customer says will register. Here is also where cultural difference plays a critical role. In North American culture, anger is accepted as a regrettable but understandable part of human nature. If one side blows his top during a conflict, when the storm is over both sides will get back to the table without too much long term repercussion. In the Chinese culture, public display of anger is a threat to harmony. Not only does it offend the other party's face, it also is evidence that you are unable to control yourself. Chinese people regard those who display anger in public as *méi yǒu xiū yǎng*, or uncivilized, something only uneducated peasants of the past would do. This does not mean Chinese people will not get angry, but they will rarely show their anger in public.

The second hurdle is the tendency to listen only to the words not the message or the feelings behind. Steven Covey, in *The Seven Habits of Highly Effective People*, discusses the five levels of listening. The first two levels, ignoring and pretending, are really not listening at all. The third level, selective listening, involves hearing only certain parts of the conversation. The fourth level, attentive listening, involves paying attention to the words being said. The fifth level, empathic listening, involves listening with an intent to understand. In Covey's words, empathic listening "gets inside another person's frame of reference." Of the five levels, perhaps empathic listening comes closest to the Chinese concept of *lǐng huì*, which means "receiving your message and my mind is in accord with your concerns."

The third hurdle is the tendency to form your response before you look at the whole picture. Once a position is formed, the rest of your listening will be focused on how to support your position instead of creatively solving the problem. This is another aspect where North American culture is different from most Asian cultures. In North America, many people start to resolve a problem or conflict with a position. Then they support their position with data, evidence and business cases. In most Asian cultures, people come to the table with information and a goal. They put the information together as if piecing a puzzle. When there are sufficient pieces put together, the final picture or solution will become clear to everyone concerned. This is a very different kind of problem solving approach.

When the customers or associates realize that you truly understand their concerns, including how they feel about the situation, the conflict is already half solved. What is left is to find a solution that is satisfactory to both parties. It is important at this point to let your associates know that you are on their side and will take care of the problem for them. In Cantonese, people often say *"Tong lay gow dim kui,"* meaning "I'll set it straight for you." It also implies, "Don't worry, you can count on me." Your customers or associates are reasonable people. They know resolving a conflict does not mean one side giving in to the other side. They are also concerned about you giving in too much in the short term and hurting the relationship with you in the long term. Thus when you say "set things straight for them," it does not mean they do not have to give in or give away anything. It means you are now standing on the same side with them to resolve the problem together.

Once your customer or associate knows you are on his side, he will be open to your concerns. Do not present your concerns as if they are your problems. Present them as hurdles in your effort to reach the common solution for you both. Hurdles are obstacles that can be overcome. It may require your associate's help, but the goal is for the mutual benefit of both.

There are of course times when you and your associate reach an impasse. When you sense an impasse is reached, suggest deferring the decision to a later time. Sometimes your Chinese associate may begin avoiding you, finding the flimsiest excuses not to meet with you or not returning your calls. Westerners not used to such behaviours can find them very annoying. The avoidance is in fact your associate's strategy to have a cooling off period while maintaining each other's face and harmony. At the end of the cooling off period, if the impasse is still unresolved, suggest referring the decision to a mutually respected authority.

Resolving a conflict can be a powerful way of strengthening the relationship with your Chinese associates. If you successfully resolve a problem with them and for them, they will know they can count on you the next time. They know that in all business ventures, there are always risks and complications. A good supplier and business partner is one that will stand by when a storm comes, not just protect his own interests and desert his associates in their moment of peril.

## *Ancient Chinese Business Principles*

Chinese people have been doing business for thousands of years. The Chinese patron saint of merchants is called Fàn Lì, also known as Táo Zhūgōng, who lived in the Third Century, B.C. Fàn Lì was a minister of the state of Yuè which at one time was conquered by the state of Wú. Fàn Lì master-minded the return of Yuè's king to his throne, rebuilt the country, and assisted the king in destroying the state of Wú. After the victory, Fàn Lì retired from politics, travelled far and wide, and became a merchant. Within two decades, he moved three times, and each time he became very rich in business.

Fàn Lì invented a number of business principles, which have been followed by most Chinese business people throughout the ages. To know how a Chinese business person thinks, read some of these rules. They cover everything from customer service to investment timing to credit policy:

- To operate a business, one must be hardworking and efficient.
- All expenditure must be reduced to the bare necessity.
- Be affable when dealing with people.
- Follow the times when it comes to buying and selling.
- Prices once agreed upon must be clearly stated.
- Give credit only to the people you know.
- Account books must be audited from time to time.
- Good products must be separated from inferior products.

- All goods must be arranged in an orderly fashion.
- Use only honourable people.
- Take extra care when making or receiving a payment.
- Inspect all goods on arrival.
- When payment is done by instalments, all terms of the agreement must be in writing.
- Allow no ambiguity when it comes to accounting.
- Be responsible in managing things.
- Be calm in making decisions.

It is interesting to note how many of these basic business principles are still valid today.

# Concluding Remarks

This book started with information on the Chinese culture and ended with advice about making friends with your customers. If there is one message I would like the readers to take away, it is: "Let Canadians of all origins prosper together through harmony, friendship and mutual respect." This is the philosophy behind all the words in the book. I wrote about serving Chinese customers only because that is the culture I know best. I hope readers will extend the same philosophy to customers of every heritage.

A good part of this book was written amidst the sound of my daughter's music practice. My daughter Joycelin is a young violinist with the Vancouver Youth Symphony Orchestra. One day she interrupted her practice and came to me with this question: "Who am I, a Canadian or a Chinese?"

I looked at her, and saw the likeness of myself and my wife in her face. She looks Chinese, speaks Chinese, enjoys Chinese dishes and celebrates Chinese festivals. She is unmistakably Chinese. At the same time, I also saw in her face the same pair of eyes that once filled with contentment over a hearty sugaring-off party years ago in Quebec where she was born, and the same eyes that sparkled with excitement every time she met a new friend as we moved and lived in different parts of the country. I remembered one summer as we drove across the Rockies, she and her brother Jonathan were singing "O Canada!" to the mountains, in both English and French. She is unmistakably Canadian.

At that point, instead of answering directly, I asked her: "Are you a violinist or are you a member of the orchestra?"

"Both," she said.

"In the same way," I told her, "you are both Chinese and Canadian. Chinese is your heritage, and Canada is your country."

Her question led me to a vision of a giant orchestra called Canada playing music to the world. Players in this orchestra are young and old people from all cultures. Like tunes of different instruments playing in harmony, their diversity becomes a source of inspiration for all humankind.

"Joycelin," I said, "tomorrow when you play in the concert, can you find someone among the audience who belongs to a different culture, and tell yourself that today you are performing for this person? Then after the concert, seek this person out and make friend with him or her."

"Why, Pa?" Joycelin asked.

"Because," I replied, "this is what Canada is all about."

# Appendix

# *M*andarin Pronunciation and the *Pīn Yīn* System

Unlike English words, Chinese characters are not spelt but composed of strokes. Each character is a pictorial representation of its meaning and contains no phonetic elements. To indicate how Chinese characters sound, it is necessary to use romanized symbols. A number of romanization systems exist to help pronounce Mandarin, and *pīn yīn* is the system adopted by mainland China since 1958. Note that none of these systems, including *pīn yīn*, is part of the Chinese language.

Although there are tens of thousands of different characters, many of these characters sound exactly alike. Characters that share the same sound but differ in meanings are called homonyms. Altogether, there are only about 400 different sounds in Mandarin. In *pīn yīn*, each sound comprises an initial element, a final element and a tone. All initial elements have one or more consonants while all finals have at least one vowel. There are four different tones in Mandarin. To read a character, pronounce the initial and final elements together in the appropriate tone.

For example, the Chinese word for "father" is made of the initial "b" (as in **b**ad) and the final "a" (as in f**a**ther). The tone for the word is the 4th tone (low pitch). Pronouncing *ba* together in the 4th tone will give you the sound meaning father in Mandarin.

## *Initial elements*

These initials are pronounced as indicated. You will note the similarity between them and the English phonetic system in many cases. However, note the following major exceptions: Q, X, Zh.

| *Initial* | *As in* | *Initial* | *As in* |
|-----------|---------|-----------|---------|
| B | *b*oy | P | *p*ut |
| C | i*ts* | Q | *ch*ew |
| Ch | *ch*ange | R | *r*um |
| D | *d*og | S | *s*end |
| F | *f*an | Sh | *sh*ow |
| G | *g*um | T | *t*oe |
| H | *h*all | W | *w*ide |
| J | *j*eep | X | *sh*eet |
| K | *k*eep | Y | *y*ou |
| L | *l*aw | Z | a*dz*e |
| M | *m*an | Zh | *j*aw |
| N | *n*ew | | |

## Final elements

The following finals are used in *pīn yīn*, again pronounced as indicated.

| Finals | As in | Finals | As in |
|--------|-------|--------|-------|
| a | f*a*ther | iong | y*ung* |
| ai | *ai*sle | iu | d*ew* |
| an | kh*an* | o | *awe* |
| ang | *oun*ce | ong | f*ung*us |
| ao | *ow*l | ou | th*ough* |
| e | b*u*t | u | r*u*de |
| ei | *ei*ght | ü | fe*u*d |
| en | th*un*der | ua | *wa*sabi |
| eng | s*ung* | uai | *wi*fe |
| er | *ar*e | uan | San *Juan* |
| i | *ea*t | uang | l*ong* |
| ia | *ya*hoo | ue | min*ue*tte |
| ian | y*en* | ui | *we*ep |
| iang | y*ah-ng* | | (1st and 2nd tone) |
| iao | m*iao*w | ui | w*ay* |
| ie | y*es* | | (3rd and 4th tone) |
| in | t*in* | un | *un*til |
| ing | k*ing* | uo | *wa*ll |

## Tones

Mandarin is a tone sensitive language. Words having the same initial and final elements but differing in tone will carry very different meanings. Following the example of the word *ba* used earlier, recall that the word for father is pronounced in the 4th tone. If the same word is pronounced in the 1st tone, it can mean, among other things, the numeral 8. Using the second tone, it can mean "to pull," and using the 3rd tone, "target."

The four principal tones are denoted by different symbols written over the word. The first two tones are above while the third and fourth tones are below the middle pitch. To get an idea of the proper tone to be used, try to say "oh" in the circumstances described in the table below:

| Tone | Symbol | Explanation | Say "oh" as used in |
|------|--------|-------------|---------------------|
| 1st | ō | High monotone | expression of excitement |
| 2nd | ó | Rising | expression of curiosity |
| 3rd | ǒ | Falling then rising | expression of doubt |
| 4th | ò | Falling | expression of disappointment |

# References

## Chapter One

Chiang, Wei-kuo et al. *History of Wars in China.* Taipei, 1981.

Griffith, J.P. *China: The Land and the People.* New York: Gallery Books, 1988.

Latourette, K.S. *The Chinese, Their History and Culture.* New York: MacMillan, 1964.

Nothiger, Andreas. *World History Chart.* Hemlock Printers, Burnaby, B.C., 1989.

Parker, G. ed. *The Times Illustrated History of the World.* UK: Times Books, 1995.

Smith, Bradley and Weng, Wan-go. *China: A History in Art.* Harper and Row, 1972.

Xu, M.Y., ed. *Shi Ba Shi Lue.* Tainan: Da Zhong Bookstore, 1975.

## Chapter Two

Aikman, David. *Pacific Rim: Area of Change, Area of Opportunity.* Toronto: Little Brown & Co., 1986.

DeMont, John. "A Capitalist Road: Mainland Chinese are Pouring Millions into Canadian Real Estate and Resources." *Maclean's* 24 April, 1989. p.30.

DeMont, J. and T.Fennell. *Hong Kong Money: How Chinese Families and Fortunes are Changing Canada.* Toronto: Key Porter Books, 1989.

Hong Kong. *Hong Kong 1995: A Review of 1994.* Hong Kong: Hong Kong Government Publications Centre, 1995.

Huang, E. and J. Lawrence. *Hong Kong: The Portraits of Power.* Toronto: Little, Brown & Co., 1995.

Lethbridge, D.G., ed. *The Business Environment in Hong Kong.* Hong Kong: Oxford University Press, 1984.

Perkins, Dwight. "Completing China's Move to the Market." *Journal of Economic Perspectives*, Vol 8(2), Spring, 1994.

Rabushkka, Alvin. *The New China: Comparative Economic Development in Mainland China, Taiwan and Hong Kong.* San Francisco: Westview Press, 1987.

Shipp, Steve. *Hong Kong, China: A Political History of the British Crown Colony's Transfer to Chinese Rule.* McFarland & Co., 1995.

Sung, Yun Wing. *The China Hong Kong Connection: The Key to China's Open Door Policy.* New York: Cambridge, 1991.

Tung, R.L. "People's Republic of China." *Comparative Management.* Ballinger Publishers, 1988.

White, Gordon. *Riding the Tiger: The Politics of Economic Reform in Post-Mao China.* Stanford: Stanford University Press, 1993.

## Chapter Three

Berry, J.W. Acculturation as Varieties of Adaptation. In A.M. Padilla, ed., *Acculturation: Theory, Models and Some New Findings.* Boulder, CO: Westview Press, 1980.

Berry, J.W. "Psychological Adaptation of Foreign Students." *Intercultural Counselling and Assessment: Global Perspective.* Eds. R.J. Samuda, N.A. Wolfgang. C.J. Hogrefe Inc., 1985.

Berry, John, et al. *Cross-cultural Psychology: Research and Applications.* Cambridge: Cambridge University Press, 1992.

Berry, John, ed. *Ethnicity and Culture in Canada: the Research Landscape.* Toronto: University of Toronto Press, 1994.

Bridges, William. *Transitions: Making Sense of Life's Changes._* Reading, MA: Addison-Wesley, 1980.

Chan, Anthony. *Gold Mountain: The Chinese in the New World.* Vancouver: New Star Books, 1983.

Farrow, Moira. "Immigrants' Spending Habits 'Change.'" *Vancouver Sun.* December 2, 1994.

Huang, Evelyn. *Chinese Canadians: Voices from a Community.* Vancouver: Douglas & McIntyre, 1992.

Irwin, Paul. *Asian Canadians: Canada's Hidden Advantage.* Vancouver: Asia Pacific Foundation of Canada, 1995.

Lai, David Chuenyau, ed. *Challenges for Chinese Canadians in the 90s.* Proceedings of the National Conference in Winnipeg, March 22-24, 1991.

Neuwith, G., S. Jones & J. Eyton. *Immigration Settlement Indicators: A Feasibility Study.* Ottawa: Employment and Immigration Canada, 1989.

Neuwith, G., S. Jones & J. Eyton. *A Source Book for Orientation, Language and Settlement Workers.* Ottawa: Employment and Immigration Canada, 1991.

Ting-Toomey, S. "Toward a Theory of Conflict and Culture," in W.Gudykunst, L. Steward, & S. Tin-Toomey, eds., *Communication , Culture and Organizational Processes.* Beverley Hills: Sage, 1985.

Tymo, D. et al. *Settlements in the 1990s: An Overview of the Needs of New Immigrants in the Lower Mainland and Fraser Valley.* Vancouver: Immigration Services Society of B.C., 1993.

Yee, Paul. *Saltwater City:An Illustrated History of the Chinese in Vancouver.* Vancouver: Douglas & McIntyre, 1988.

Yee, Paul. *Hope and Struggle: Chinese in Canada.* Vancouver: Umbrella Press, 1995.

## *Chapter Four*

Bond, Michael Harris. *Beyond the Chinese Face: Insights from Psychology.* Oxford University Press, 1991.

Lee, Kuan Yew. "Culture is Destiny," *Foreign Affairs*, March/April, 1994.

Hofstede, Geert. "The Cultural Relativity of Organizational Practices and Theories." *Journal of International Business Studies*, UWO Business School, 1983.

Hofstede, G. And M.H. Bond. "The Confucius Connection: From Cultural Roots to Economic Growth." *Organizational Dynamics*,

Spring, 1988.

Ting-Toomey, Stella. "Managing Intercultural Conflicts Effectively." *Communicating Interculturally: Becoming Competent.* Ed. L. Samovar and R. Porter. Belmont, CA: Wadsworth, 1994.

## *Chapter Five*

Canston, Richard. *The Buddha in Daily Life: An Introduction to the Buddha.* London: Rider, 1995.

Claxton, Guy. *The Heart of Buddhism: Practical Wisdom for an Agitated World.* Northamptonshire, England: Crucible, 1990.

Cleary, Thomas F. *The Essential Tao: An Initiation into the Heart of Taoism Through the Authentic Tao Te Ching and the Inner Teachings of Chuan-tzu.* San Francisco: Harper, 1992.

Confucius. *The Analects of Confucius.* Trans. Lun Yu. London: George Allen & Unwin, 1971.

Confucius. *The Essential Confucius: The Heart of Confucius' Teaching.* Trans. Lun Yu. San Francisco: Harper, 1992.

Kohn, Livia. *The Taoist Experience: An Anthology.* Albany, New York: State University of New York Press, 1993.

Lao Tsu. *Tao Te Ching.* Translated by Gia-Fu Feng and Jane English. New York: Vintage Books, 1972.

Rossbach, S. *Feng Shui: The Chinese Art of Placement.* New York: E.P. Dutton, 1983.

Smith, D.H. *Chinese Religions.* London: Weidenfeld & Nicolson, 1968.

Tu, Wai-ming. *Centrality and Commonality: An Essay on Confucianism.* Albany, New York: State University of New York Press, 1989.

Walters, Derek. *Feng Shui: Perfect Placing for Your Happiness and Prosperity.* Singapore: Asiapac Books, 1992.

## Chapter Six

Law, Jones. *Chinese Festivals in Hong Kong*. Hong Kong: South China Morning Post, 1982.

Latsch, Marie-Luise. *Chinese Traditional Festivals*. Beijing: New World Press, 1984.

Gee, J. Karen. *A Book of Chinese Festivals*. Osoyoos, B.C.: Steam R.R. Publication, 1989.

## Chapter Seven

Statistics Canada. *Ethnic Origin*. Cat. #93-315, 1993.

Citizenship and Immigration Canada. *Into the Twenty-first Century: A Strategy for Immigration and Citizenship*. Ministry of Supply and Services Canada, 1994.

Lynn, Jennifer. "Approaching Diversity." *Marketing Magazine*, July 3/10, 1995.

DJC Research. *The Chinese Consumer in Canada*. Toronto: DJC Research, 1995.

## Chapter Eight

Kotler, P. *Marketing Management*. New Jersey: Prentice Hall, 1994.

Thompson, A. A. Jr., and A.J. Strickland III. *Crafting & Implementing Strategy*. Richard D. Erwin Inc., 1995.

## Chapter Nine

Ford, A. "An Ethnic Feast: Business Cash in on Rich Market." *The Province*. August 16, 1992.

Gayle, M. "Specialty Markets to Cater to Asians." *The Province*. May 14, 1993. A52.

Gill, R. "Many Cultures, Many Consumers." *Vancouver Sun*. October 24, 1991.

Griffin, K. "Crossing the Line." *The Vancouver Sun*. September 15,

1990. E4-E5.

Papers presented at the Multicultural Marketing Symposium, *Marketing Magazine*, Vancouver, December, 1994.

Scotland, R. "Hong Kong Arrivals Make Quality No. 1." *Financial Post*. June 22, 1992.

Vincent, I. "Chasing After the Ethnic Consumer." *Globe and Mail*. September 18, 1995. A6.

Wanless, T. "Firms reach out to ethnic consumers." *The Province*. November 7, 1997. A46.

Wong, S. "Wake up and smell the tea." *Business in Vancouver*. Nov. 16-22, 1993.

## Chapter Ten

DuPont, M. Kay. *Business Etiquette and Professionalism*. Los Altos, California: Crisp Publications, 1990.

Pachter, Barbara. *Complete Business Etiquette Handbook*. Prentice-Hall, 1995.

Seligman, S.D. *Dealing with the Chinese*. New York: Warner Books, 1989.

Wenzhong H. And C.L. Grove. *Encountering the Chinese*. Yarmouth, Maine: Intercultural Press, 1991.

## Chapter Eleven

Chaney, L.H. and J.S. Martin. *Intercultural Business Communication*. Englewood Cliff, New Jersey: Prentice Hall, 1995.

Phillips, C.H. *China Beckons: An Insight to the Culture and National Language*. Edmonton, Alberta: University of Alberta Press, 1993.

## Chapter Twelve

Chu, Chin-Ning. *The Asian Mind Game: Unlocking the Hidden Agenda of the Asian Business Culture: A Westerner's Survival Manual*. New York: Rawson, 1991.

De Mente, Boye Lafayette. *Chinese Etiquette & Ethics in Business.* Chicago: NTC Business Books, 1994.

Greenberg, Jeanne. *What It Takes to Succeed in Sales.* Homewood, Ill.: Dow Jones-Irwin, 1990.

Hill, N. and E.H. Keown. *Succeed and Grow Rich Through Persuasion.* New York: Ballantine Books, 1970.

Schiffman, Stephan. *The 25 Most Common Sales Mistakes and How to Avoid Them.* Holbrook, Mass: Adams Pub., 1995.

Seligman, S.D. *Dealing with the Chinese.* New York: Warner Books, 1989.

Smith, R.E. *Psychology.* St. Paul, MN: West Publishing, 1993, p.371.

## *Chapter Thirteen*

Carnegie, Dale. *How to Win Friends and Influence People.* New York: Pocket Books, Revised edition, 1981.

Covey, S. *The Seven Habits of Highly Effective People.* New York: Simon & Schuster, 1989.

Cragg, Claudia. *Hunting with the Tigers: Doing Business with Hong Kong, Indonesia, S. Korea, Malaysia, the Philippines, Singapore, Taiwan, Thailand and Vietnam.* San Diego: Pfeiffer, 1993.

Naisbitt, J. *Megatrends Asia: Eight Megatrends that Are Reshaping Our World.* New York: Simon & Schuster, 1996.

Seligman, S.D. *Dealing with the Chinese.* New York: Warner Books, 1989.

"The Chinese in Canada." *The Financial Post*, November 24, 1995. C1-C12.

# Suggested Readings on Related Issues

## About the future of Asia

Naisbitt, J. *Megatrends Asia: Eight Megatrends that Are Reshaping Our World.* New York: Simon & Schuster, 1996.

## About the prospect of Hong Kong after 1997

Huang, E. and J. Lawrence. *Hong Kong: The Portraits of Power.* Toronto: Little, Brown & Co., 1995.

## About business concerns of Asian Canadians

Irwin, Paul. *Asian Canadians: Canada's Hidden Advantage.* Vancouver: Asia Pacific Foundation of Canada, 1995.

## About Chinese business ethics and etiquette

De Mente, Boye Lafayette. *Chinese Etiquette & Ethics in Business.* Chicago: NTC Business Books, 1994.

## About doing business in China

Seligman, S.D. *Dealing with the Chinese.* New York: Warner Books, 1989.

Wenzhong H. And C.L. Grove. *Encountering the Chinese.* Yarmouth, Maine: Intercultural Press, 1991.

Hinkelman, Edward G. ed. *China Business: The Portable Encyclopedia for Doing Business with China.* San Rafael: World Trade Press, 1994.

## About doing business in Hong Kong

Hinkelman, Edward G. ed. *Hong Kong Business: The Portable Encyclopedia for Doing Business with Hong Kong.* San Rafael: World Trade Press, 1994

## About doing business in Taiwan

Hinkelman, Edward G. ed. *Taiwan Business: The Portable Encyclopedia for Doing Business with Taiwan.* San Rafael: World Trade Press, 1994

# Index

316

# ◈ S.U.C.C.E.S.S.
## Committed to Serving the Community

S.U.C.C.E.S.S. (the United Chinese Community Enrichment Services Society), was incorporated in 1973 as a non-profit charitable organization with the mission of helping new immigrants to adjust and integrate. It bridges cultural, linguistic and social gaps between new Canadians and the mainstream society.

In its 22 years of operation, S.U.C.C.E.S.S. has developed a comprehensive range of services to assist clients in overcoming language and cultural barriers and achieve self-reliance so that they may contribute fully to the Canadian society. It is the largest social service agency in the Chinese community in British Columbia, now serving 150,000 clients every year at eight locations in the Lower Mainland.

The Society also promotes the vision of multiculturalism. Programs have been adjusted and services diversified from serving the Chinese community initially to providing support and services to newcomers of other ethnic background.

The outstanding contribution of S.U.C.C.E.S.S. has been widely recognized and as a result, it was granted the Citation of Citizenship Award by the Canadian Government in 1994.

# S.U.C.C.E.S.S. OFFICES

## Head Office
87 East Pender Street,
Vancouver, B.C., V6A 1S9
Tel: (604) 684 - 1628
Fax: (604) 684 - 3328

## West Broadway Office
#501-1788 West Broadway St.,
Vancouver, B.C., V6J 1Y1
Tel: (604) 732 - 3278
Fax: (604) 732 - 9818

## Fraser Office
5836 Fraser Street,
Vancouver, B.C., V5W 2Z5
Tel: (604) 324 - 1900
Fax: (604) 321 - 1955

## Mandarin Service Centre
5540 Cambie Street,
Vancouver, B.C., V5Z 3A2
Tel: (604) 323 - 0901
Fax: (604) 323 - 0902

## Richmond Office
#220 - 7000 Minoru Blvd.,
Richmond, B.C., V6Y 3Z5
Tel: (604) 279 - 7180
Fax: (604) 279 - 7188

## Burnaby-Coquitlam Office
#2A - 555 North Rd.,
Coquitlam, B.C., V3J 1N8
Tel: (604) 936 - 5900
Fax: (604) 936 - 7280

## C. A. N. N.
#280 - 8191 Westminster Highway,
Richmond, B.C., V6X 1A7
Tel: (604) 270 - 0077
Fax: (604) 270 - 6008

## Tri-City Office
#114 Westwood Mall,
3000 Lougheed Hwy.,
Coquitlam, B.C., V3B 1C5
Tel: (604) 941 - 8892
Fax: (604) 941 - 8297